Lilli
Jenn

FORTUNE & FENG SHUI

BOAR

2021

KONSEPBOOKS

ASTROLOGY . FENG SHUI . INSPIRATIONS

Fortune & Feng Shui 2021 Boar

by *Lillian Too* and *Jennifer Too*
© 2021 Konsep Lagenda Sdn Bhd

Text © 2021 Lillian Too and Jennifer Too
Photographs and illustrations © Konsep Lagenda Sdn Bhd
Cover Art © Josh Yeo Zhu Lin

The moral right of the authors to be identified as authors of this book has been asserted.

Published by KONSEP LAGENDA SDN BHD (223 855)
Kuala Lumpur 59100 Malaysia

For more Konsep books, go to *www.lillian-too.com* or *www.wofs.com*
To report errors, please send a note to errors@konsepbooks.com
For general feedback, email feedback@konsepbooks.com

Notice of Liability

The information in this book is distributed on an "As Is" basis, without warranty. While every precaution has been taken in the preparation of the book, neither the author nor Konsep Lagenda shall have any liability to any person or entity with respect to any loss or damage caused or alleged to be caused directly or indirectly by the instructions contained in this book.

ISBN 978-967-2929-04-8
Published in Malaysia, September 2020

BOAR 2021

BIRTH YEAR	WESTERN CALENDAR DATES	AGE	KUA NUMBER MALES	KUA NUMBER FEMALES
Wood Boar	4 Feb 1935 - 23 Jan1936	86	2 West Group	4 East Group
Fire Boar	22 Jan 1947 - 9 Feb 1948	74	8 West Group	7 West Group
Earth Boar	8 Feb 1959 - 27 Jan 1960	62	5/2 West Group	1 East Group
Metal Boar	27 Jan 1971 - 14 Feb 1972	50	2 West Group	4 East Group
Water Boar	13 Feb 1983 - 1 Feb 1984	38	8 West Group	7 West Group
Wood Boar	31 Jan 1995 - 18 Feb 1996	26	5/2 West Group	1 East Group
Fire Boar	18 Feb 2007 - 6 Feb 2008	14	2 West Group	1 East Group

Cover Art by Josh Yeo Zhu Lin

Features a jovial Boar reminiscent of beloved "Wilbur" of E.B. White's Charlotte's Web. In 2021, the Boar enjoys two Auspicious stars – Big AND Small – a fabulous indication indeed!

CONTENTS

Chapter Five
BOAR INTERACTING WITH OTHER SIGNS 140
Boar benefits from being surrounded by the right people

Chapter Six
BOAR'S MONTHLY HOROSCOPE FOR 2021 176
Adjust your expectations and don't be in a hurry for results

Introduction to the Year 2021

Chapter 1

YEAR OF THE METAL OX

The coming year is the Year of the Metal Ox, a year when harvests are reaped as a result of old-fashioned hard work. It takes on the nature of the diligent Ox, whose finest qualities are its stability and steadfastness, the sign that symbolizes all the hard work that has to be done in order to prepare for the harvests and prosperity that follows. While the coming year can be prolific, there are few shortcuts to be had. Those who put in the hours and who match their effort with their wit will be those who reap the most from the year. This will not be a time for easy money or overnight speculative gains. It will be a year when substance wins out over panache, and when those who put emphasis on building solid foundations will prosper. One should strive to work first at what one can bring to the table, before making promises or trying to convince others of one's potential.

THE TOILING OX

This is the year of the Metal Ox, so it is one in which the Earth element of the Ox gets constantly exhausted by its heavenly stem of Metal. Earth produces Metal, so is exhausted by it. This is a year when the Ox has to constantly keep up its efforts to stay ahead. Individuals who are dedicated and disciplined will be the most effective and the most successful.

The year can be an industrious one, but only if one acts industriously. There is good progress to be made for those who consciously and actively mirror the attributes of the steady Ox. It will be a year void of lightning speed success but conscientious work pays off. It is a year that rewards hard work over talent, where practice trumps winging it.

FORMIDABLE FRIENDS AND FOES

The Ox sign makes a loyal friend but also a formidable enemy, so the year will see both sides of this coin. Competitive pressures will be tough, but those with robust teams of collaborators and allies will succeed. Factions will form and there will be both poignant friendships and daunting foes. Those that stand alone will find it difficult to navigate through the various obstacles that the year offers up.

The Paht Chee of 2021 features both a troublesome clash and a promising alliance in its earthly branch line up. There is a clash between the Ox and the Sheep in the Day Pillar, but also an encouraging connection between the Ox and the Rat in the Hour Pillar. It is a year when friendships matter, so one must work at keeping one's friends. Those that slip the net to the other side could become intimidating enemies. People will tend to hold grudges and have long memories. The advice is to avoid offending the wrong people with careless words and unthinking actions. Skins are thin and offense is taken at the smallest acts of offhandedness.

THE LEADER REIGNS SUPREME

The twelve months from February 4th 2021 to February 4th 2022 will support people in leadership positions. Those who have recently risen to high office or who were promoted last year, whether in Government or in Commerce, will feel the benefits of the year's energies. Such individuals enjoy the buoyancy of the winds and waters that translate into a powerful flow

PAHT CHEE CHART 2021

HOUR	DAY	MONTH	YEAR
壬	癸	庚	辛
Yang Water	Yin Water	Yang Metal	Yin Metal
壬子	己未	甲寅	己丑
Yang Water Rat	Yin Earth Sheep	Yang Wood Tiger	Yin Earth Ox

of auspicious heaven luck. They benefit from a special vitality that aids their decision-making. Their actions carry weight and they find it easy to garner support for what they want to do.

With the #6 Heaven Star taking center stage in the year's Flying Star chart, leaders and those in positions of power are blessed with the mantle of heaven. It instills in them great authority and effect over their charges so they will have greater ability to influence the outcome of what they are engaged in.

This year favours leaders, chiefs, bosses, managers and directors of all kinds, and in all fields.

The danger this year is that the #7 afflictive star has arrived in the NW, the sector that represents the Patriarch. With leaders so powerful and with the treacherous #7 star in its home location, this brings the risk that those in power may use their position for harm rather than for good. Leaders with strong moral ethics can effect very positive change with a big and lasting impact, but those who act on a whim could end up making disastrous decisions that affect the fortunes of many.

The presence of the Ox-Sheep clash in the chart suggests that while leaders may be powerful within their own spheres, they meet with hostility from opposing interest groups, and leaders of other nations and organizations. Different blocs will have differing agendas, and when compromises cannot be reached, there will be conflict and struggle.

On the world stage, the influence of the #7 on the leader suggests there will be much fighting energy, and even risk of war. US-China trade relations will continue to deteriorate, with effects impacting more and more nations. Worrying alliances may be formed. There will be unified groups but it will not be one unified assembly; there will be powerful diverse groups that clash and clatter.

Conspiracy theorists may well have some premise to their conjectures; this becomes ever more likely if the ominous influence of the excessive Metal in the year's chart is not strongly suppressed. All may not be what it seems to be on the surface.

THE INFLUENCE OF THE ELEMENTS

METAL *represents authority*

METAL in 2021 stands for RESOURCES, but it also stands for AUTHORITY. Unfortunately, in 2021, authority may not always be benevolent. This year there is almost too much Metal energy, and too much makes the ominous side of this element stronger. Leaders become more powerful, and power here has to potential to corrupt. Checks and balances become more important, as the year could produce leaders who make unscrupulous decisions, taking into account only their own personal agendas.

This affliction affects not just leaders on the world stage but those in one's immediate sphere as well – bosses, community leaders, mentors, teachers, parents. If this Metal energy is not kept under control, it could lead to disastrous consequences in one's personal daily life. The effects of this can feel very real and close to home.

WHAT TO DO: We suggest displaying a **red-faced Kuan Kung**, the powerful Warrior God in the home and office to protect against the excess of Metal element energy. Having this God of War and God of Wealth in the home ensures you stay on the winning side of the element luck effect. Kuan Kung will ensure you make judicious decisions that end up benefiting you and your family in the long run. Gives you courage to move forward but tempers any misplaced bravado.

Red-faced Kuan Kung with 5 victory flags

2. Wearing jewellery in precious Metals fashioned as sacred syllables and symbols transforms the effect of Metal from autocratic to benevolent. It helps keep you protected from harm and ensures you do not lose the support of the people who matter most to your prospects in life- eg. Your boss, your parents, your teachers.

WATER *represents competition*
WATER in 2021 stands for FRIENDS and FOES, which are present in equal measure. Both have an equivalent part to play in the outcomes that follow. Because the year is one of STRONG WATER, the element of Water this year needs to be treated with caution. Too much of it could tip the scales over, attracting fierce rivalry and underhand tactics by one's competition, rather than cultivating strong allies that stay loyal.

This year it becomes especially important to carry protective amulets that guard against betrayal and disloyalty. Carrying an image of **Kuan Kung with Anti-Betrayal Amulet** will help protect against becoming a victim of these energies. Always give others suitable respect, and don't disregard the dangers of allies changing sides. If the incentive becomes attractive enough, they will. Don't take anything too personally if you can adopt the stoic outlook of the Ox where you make the most of the opportunities open to you without complaining too much what is fair or not fair. You can effectively buffer against many of the pitfalls of the year.

THE COLOR BLUE – Blacks and blues stand for Water energy. While water to the Chinese traditionally represents money, this year it also signifies competition. Using too much of this color this year holds the danger of fueling rivalry and competitiveness amongst one's peers. Do not don too much black, and when you do, try to add a splash of color to neutralize its more sinister effects. Place the **Celestial Water Dragon** in the home to keep this element under control.

FIRE *brings wealth*

FIRE in 2021 stands for WEALTH LUCK. This is the element that appears to be completely missing from the year's chart and thus is the one we must actively work at replacing. There is hidden wealth brought by the Tiger, but this needs a trigger for it to be actualized. We suggest wearing the color red in free abandon this year. Remember, this is the Year of the Ox, an Earth sign whose inner vitality gets spurred on by the wonderful energy of Fire.

THE COLOR RED - Red to the Chinese is always considered lucky. It is a color of celebration and carnival. It is traditionally used in all auspicious occasions, and as we move into the new year of 2021, it is especially important to wear plenty of red! For the first 15 days of the Lunar New Year, we recommend getting yourself a red outfit for each day. Keep up this ritual through the entire 15 days of celebrations to ensure its effects can get you through the year. This is an excellent way to "fuel up" for the year, as it is a year when the element of Fire is glaringly missing.

In the home, keep the lights bright throughout the year. Change your lightbulbs whenever they start to flicker or lose energy, and don't try to save on the electricity bill by constantly turning off the lights! It is far more important to work at keeping this element properly energized through the year. Don't be penny wise and pound foolish. Lights represent Fire energy, and Fire energy represents wealth and prosperity in 2021.

NEW WEALTH WALLET: Each year it is an extremely lucky ritual to get yourself a new wallet and transfer some money from your old wallet over to your new one, while adding in some brand new notes (best if from cash received as a Chinese New Year ang pow, or from one's latest drawn salary or bonus). You can also keep an image of the **Wealth God Sitting on**

a Tiger in the form of a Gold Card inside your wallet; very auspicious as the Tiger is the sign that brings hidden wealth to the year.

Each year we design a wallet to vibrate and sync with the energies of the year, and for 2021, our wealth wallet features the stock market bull. It is the Year of the Ox and the Wall Street Bull is a most auspicious

symbolic cousin of the sign of the year. The Wall Street Bull represents your investments going up, and your asset wealth growing.

We also have the **Asset Wealth Bull with Wealth Amulet** which will attract wealth-generating luck to any home which invites it in. Display prominently in the West where the *Star of Current Prosperity* has flown to this year or on your desk in front of you where you work. The idea is to see it daily and its subliminal effects will magically influence your actions and ability to attract wealth luck into your life.

WOOD *brings growth*

WOOD is the element that stands for growth. In 2021, it also signifies intelligence and creativity. It is what brings fresh new ideas to the mix, encouraging a blossoming of imagination and ingenuity. As we foray further into the new decade, old ideas will increasingly lose appeal and old technologies become obsolete with increasing speed. These need to be replaced and they will, and it will be those who can dream up the new ideas, methods, designs and technologies that will profit.

For the individual looking at making it in a rapidly changing world, it will be enhanced creativity and thinking outside the box that will help you. Surround yourself with the vibrant energy of plants and greenery, invite fresh flowers displayed in auspicious vases into your living space. If you live in a modern skyscraper city where feasting on green is difficult or unusual, look for ways to introduce indoor gardens into your home and office space, take regular time to visit parks and gardens, or make time to visit the countryside to refuel and recharge your senses with the power of nature.

THE COLOR GREEN – Greens of all kinds represent innovation and vision in 2021. Fill your wardrobe with lots of this color in emerald green, lime green, neon green, shamrock, chartreuse, sage, seafoam… all of these will inject your wardrobe with a fresh dash of inspiration and will attract wonderfully inspired energies into your aura. Green this year is very lucky and brings to the wearer a new lease of life. If you have been feeling dull, uninspired or at a crossroads, introducing a pop of bright green into what you wear or carry will give you the boost you need to change track, get moving, get started. It is the "energizing" colour of the year and should be made use of liberally and profusely.

TEND TO YOUR GARDEN: There's nothing that invokes better yang Wood energy than thriving plants and greenery. Make a trip to your local nursery and bring home some vibrant new plants to add to your garden. If you live in an apartment, introduce some live potted plants into your living space. This will stir up the creative juices in you needed to dream up new ideas and to hatch ingenious strategies for your work and in your life.

EARTH *brings power & influence*
EARTH in the Year of the Ox is the intrinsic element of the animal sign of the year. It is the element that symbolizes stability, strength and permanence. It is the element that ensures that however crazy the energy gets, however quickly the world changes around us, we can dig our heels deep and stay grounded with

our values and our visions intact. Earth energy will prevent us being light-eared and light-headed, or easily influenced. In 2021, the element of EARTH also signifies recognition and power. It brings the luck of rank and position, and boosts one's chances when it comes to promotion and upward mobility, whether in one's career or in any climb to the top of any organization. Earth energy brings you influence and command and will make people listen to you.

EARTH COLORS – Wearing shades of earth tones brings you respect and makes people listen to you. It keeps you rational and well-balanced and envelops you with an aura of dependability. An excellent color group to use when you need others to take you seriously. Earth colors include yellow, orange, beige and cream, in all their shades. Wear such colors when you feel you need others to take notice of you, when you want to boost your influence over others and when you need people to listen to you. Those of you ambitious for your career to get a boost will benefit greatly from making use of earth colors.

THE 24 MOUNTAINS CHART OF 2021

The compass wheel around which the animals are positioned contain 24 mountains, which attract different stars each year. The overall fortunes of the year get enhanced or disabled depending on which

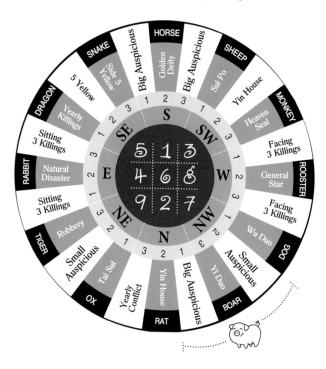

stars settle into which corners. Some years will have more auspicious stars, and some less, and their positions around the wheel impact on each animal sign differently.

THE LUCK OF BIG & SMALL AUSPICIOUS

One of the luckiest indications from this chart are the Big and Small Auspicious Stars, and in 2021, we have 5 of such stars making an appearance. The year enjoys three *Big Auspicious* stars and two *Small Auspicious* stars. The animal signs that benefit from these are the **Horse**, **Snake**, **Sheep**, **Rat**, **Boar**, the **Dog**, **Ox** and **Tiger**. The locations of these stars are spread out giving the above animal signs the potential to seize opportunities that come their way.

The sign that benefits most from this indication is the **HORSE**. The Horse enjoys two Big Auspicious stars, which suggests that after two difficult years, this sign is ready to take flight. The free-spirited Horse person can finally seize what it has been grappling after; this is a year when this sign can take risks and put wholehearted effort behind their passions. It is a year when the Horse should not rest on its laurels, because the big time has arrived.

The other signs enjoying Big Auspicious are the **Snake** and **Sheep**, and the **Rat** and **Boar**. These signs also have the potential to go after big dreams and, to

 realize big ambitions they may have been harboring. For these signs, opportunities will be plentiful. Success comes for those who are hungry and resolute. Remember that this year, results do not come immediately, so one must not get discouraged if the path to actualization seems long or even impossible. The winners will be those with the staying power to keep at it and stay the course. Hold on to your dreams, and don't change your mind at every setback. Trust in your instincts and passions, and don't give power to those who disturb your mind or pour cold water on your ideas.

While the Stars of Big Auspicious bring really fabulous blessings, so do the Stars of Small Auspicious. These have the same effect as their big brother stars, but they bring success in smaller measures and in stages. The signs enjoying Small Auspicious this year are the **Ox**, **Tiger**, **Dog** and **Boar**. For these signs, they are likely to meet with small successes that form the stepping stones to bigger success later on. For these signs, this is a year for building firm foundations and laying out the pathway for future triumphs.

Small Auspicious brings end goals that hold slightly longer time trajectories, but accompanied with the same staying power, success does ultimately come. Learn to celebrate the smellet of wins and stay clearheaded about your ultimate goals. If you constantly step back to examine the bigger picture, you will not lose sight of why you are doing what you're doing.

ENHANCER: Remember that *Stars of Big and Small Auspicious* bring the potential of great fortune, but to enjoy their benefits to the fullest, they need to be enhanced. Each year then, we design a Big Auspicious Enhancer to kickstart the very positive effects of these stars. This year, all animal signs benefit from displaying the **Six Birds Auspicious Multiplier**. This activator featuring an I-Ching coin with six birds and the auspicious amulet enhancer brings new opportunities. The 6 birds activates the #6 Heaven Star that rules the year's Lo Shu chart. The number 6 is the number of the heavens, which unlocks the celestial hand of the Gods. Display this potent activator in a place where you can see it often – either in a prominent place in the home, or in front of you on your work desk.

6 Birds Auspicious Multiplier. Unlocks the Big Auspicious luck of the year.

LUCK FROM THE HEAVENS

Two stars that further magnify the luck of the heavens are the *Golden Deity Star* and the *Star of the Heavenly Seal*. These land in the location of the **Horse** and the **Monkey**, bringing these two signs the luck of celestial fortunes. For these two signs, help comes without having to seek it. They enjoy the patronage of powerful mentors with many wishing to help them. They also have better instincts and can trust their own judgment more. For the Horse, as it also enjoys two Big Auspicious stars, little can go wrong as long as it stays judicious and diligent. The Monkey however needs to employ its trademark cunning to make the most of the Heaven Seal; it has to dodge the Yin House and Facing 3 Killings, but its main 24 Mountain star influence is extremely positive.

To make the most of these stars, we recommend that the Horse and Monkey invite in a **Golden Deity** into the home. Any Buddha, God or holy figure in line with your own faith will work. We particularly love **Kuan Yin, the Goddess of Mercy**, revered by Chinese all around the world. She is the female personification of the compassionate Buddha and brings wealth, health and happiness and protection from harm.

Kuan Yin

THE GENERAL STAR

The **Rooster** enjoys the General Star, which brings it power and authority, but unfortunately also fuels its short fuse and hot temper. But the Rooster this year has the very lucky #8 star, which enhances its fortunes and intrinsic energy. The Rooster as a sign does not suffer fool's gladly, so all these indications point to a Rooster that reigns supreme in 2021, but one who may be insufferable to those it considers "beneath" them, whether in intelligence or in status. To make the most of this star, all Roosters this year benefit from displaying the **Power Ru Yi**, the scepter of authority which boosts its command as boss or leader, while ensuring no disgruntled subordinates try to make trouble, or rivals rise up to try to displace it.

Star of the Yin House

This star brings danger of sickness and disease, and a general lack of energy to those it afflicts. It is particularly dangerous if one is already ill or elderly, or with other heavy afflictions indicated in their charts. This year, there are two Yin House stars and these arrive in the SW and North, affecting the **Sheep**, **Monkey** and **Rat**. All three of these signs are advised to take more care this year when it comes to health, well-being and safety. We strongly suggest that these signs carry protective amulets to shield them from the influence of malevolent spirits that may wreak havoc in their lives. Any of the **seed syllables Om, Ah or**

OM   AH   HUM

Hum will invoke the presence of the mighty Buddha, establishing a firm spiritual circumference of protection around the wearer.

If ill health is of particular concern, we recommend wearing and displaying health amulets. The **Wu Lou**, **Garuda Bird**, and the **Healing Deer**, bring precious cosmic protection. The deer is especially wonderful; this animal has always been associated with health, strength and vigor. It is also the animal that holds the solution to good health when all other methods have not seemed to work. There are many folk legends associated with the deer in all cultures, but in Chinese mythology, the deer is almost always shown accompanying Sau, the divine God of Longevity.

Healing Deer

The Robbery Star

This star brings money loss and betrayal and especially affects the **Tiger** in 2021. Those born under this sign need to be especially mindful not to get taken in by con men and getting cheated by others. There is higher chance of getting conned into undertaking bad investments. Business partners and associates could prove untrustworthy. It is also very important whenever one has this affliction to take care of personal safety. Robberies, muggings, petty thieves and street crime become more of a danger. This star also brings risk of becoming a victim of chance or collateral damage in somebody else's fight.

To counter this negative star, you need the image of the **Blue Rhino and Elephant** in the home, and you MUST carry the **Anti Robbery Amulet**. This protects against losing money and possessions. It is also important to protect against personal harm and injury; wear protective amulet at all times! Females in particular should avoid venturing out alone late at night or putting themselves under unnecessary risk; they should carry the **Nightspot Protection Amulet** for protection against petty crime.

Yearly Conflict & Yearly Killings

These stars bring obstacles to everything you do, making it difficult to make meaningful progress. These are the stars that can discourage you from remaining steadfast and keeping on your intended path. It throws up unexpected snags and hitches, and when left unchecked, can overwhelm one with feelings of depression and anxiety. These are negative stars that gather the slings and arrows of misfortune hurling them your way with some measure of ferocity. It is as such extremely important to take note of their location each year and take definite steps to neutralize them.

In 2021, the Yearly Killings star has landed in the **Dragon**'s location of SE1, and the Yearly Conflict Star visits the N3 sector, affecting the animal signs of **Rat** and **Ox**.

The *Yearly Killings Star* is deadlier and needs immediate action – we suggest that all Dragon-born and all those whose bedrooms or main door location are in the SE carry the **28 Hums Protection Wheel** and invite in the **Buddha image of Nangsi Zilnon Guru Rinpoche**. He is the warrior Buddha who completely overcomes all types of obstacles brought by the Yearly Killings.

28 Hums
Protection
Wheel

The *Yearly Conflict Star* makes everyone want to fight with you, bringing opposition to your ideas and making it difficult to see your projects through. Working in teams becomes especially difficult. At work, this could mean difficult colleagues and fierce politicking by workplace rivals. Those afflicted by this star could find themselves spending the better part of their time dodging potshots rather than focusing on their work. It makes work life very unpleasant, and the effects of this star can also permeate one's social and private life. This negative star arrives in the N3 sector affecting all whose main door or bedroom or office are located in this part of the home or office, and it affects Rat and Ox born people. Those affected by this affliction need to carry protection amulets and display the relevant cures. The **Dorje Drolo Scorpion Amulet** is especially helpful in this regard.

Natural Disaster Star

This star arrives in the East sector, affecting those who spend much time in this part of the home. This is the star that puts in you in harm's way – being at the wrong place at the wrong time. It brings all manner of natural misfortune including floods, fires, earthquakes, tsunamis, viruses and disease. If you are afflicted by this star, you MUST carry spiritual protection. ALL East-facing homes benefit from inviting in a statue of **Guru Rinpoche**, and all who live in East-facing homes should wear the **Bhrum Pendant** which protects against all kinds of harm, illness, accidents and avoidable misfortune.

LUCK OF THE 12 ANIMAL SIGNS

Every animal sign is affected by a host of factors which change each year, producing a different basket of combinations which influence each individual sign's luck differently. Aside from the animal sign year you were born under, there are additional factors affecting your luck, but viewed together with these indications, anyone can alter the course of their lives and make intelligent decisions to maximize luck through any given year.

Here we summarize the broad outlook for the different animal signs, and in later chapters of this book, we go into greater depth and detail on what all of this means for you personally, depending on your heavenly stem, your home direction, your lunar mansion and your compatibilities.

The **HORSE** is blessed with extremely fortunate indications with the double *stars of Big Auspicious* and the *Star of Golden Deity* brought by the 24 Mountains Compass of 2021. This sign has great good fortune coming, which should more than make up for the unfortunate stars it had to endure in the last two years. The Horse is an energetic and restless sign full of passion and appetite for adventure, but the last couple of years will have made it difficult for it to pursue its desires. This year changes all of this; the Horse person will feel like a cloud has lifted, and as the year progresses, things get better and better. There are no unlucky indications at all, and the Victory Star #1 promises some very exciting new developments in the Horse's life.

The Horse should boost its fortunes with the **6 Birds Auspicious Multiplier** and benefits from displaying the **Desktop Flag of Victory** in its vicinity.

The **MONKEY** and **ROOSTER** are the signs enjoying the luckiest element luck indications. These two Metal signs have superlative Life Force and Spirit Essence, suggesting an inner determination that is unwavering. These signs know exactly what it is they want and how to go about getting it. Both Monkey and Rooster are known for their innate intelligence and ingenuity, and their already immense brainpower gets a big boost this year. The Monkey in particular enjoys very promising "success" luck; not only can it get what it wants, it receives plenty of recognition to go along with it too!

The **Rooster** can boost success luck by surrounding itself with the presence of the **Victorious Windhorse Carrying a Jewel**, as can the Monkey. Both these signs also have excellent indications from the 24 Mountains, with Monkey enjoying the *Heaven Seal* and Rooster benefitting from the *General Star*. The Monkey should carry the **Dragon Heavenly Seal Amulet** and the Rooster needs the **Ru Yi**.

Dragon
Heavenly
Seal Amulet

The sign that gets hit by the *Five Yellow* this year are the **DRAGON** and **SNAKE**. This indicates that these signs need to watch that the *wu wang* does not bring misfortune their way. The Five Yellow of 2021 sits in a Wood sector, which suggests it is NOT a deadly Five Yellow; nevertheless, the obstacles it brings can cause life to feel very unpleasant indeed and it should be strongly subdued.

 Dragon and Snake this year need to carry the **Five Element Pagoda Amulet with Tree of Life** to combat the afflictive energy, turning obstacles into productive challenges, and transforming unfortunate outcomes into promising ones. Both Dragon and Snake are signs that thrive in adversity, gaining strength and shrewdness when the going gets tough. And the *wu wang* of this year can be metamorphosed into positive rather than negative results. The Snake should have the **6 Birds Auspicious Multiplier**, while the Dragon needs the **28 Hums Protection Wheel**.

The WOOD ELEMENT SIGNS of **TIGER** and **RABBIT** both enjoy very good element indications but need to boost success luck with the **Victorious Windhorse**. The Tiger benefits from *Small Auspicious*, and direct access to the hidden wealth of the year, but the Rabbit needs to do more work to boost its prosperity potential. The Tiger should display the **6 Birds Auspicious Multiplier** while the Rabbit MUST carry the **Three Celestial Shields Amulet** to stay protected against the 3 Killings affliction that affects it this year.

The WATER ELEMENT SIGNS of **RAT** and **BOAR** are the most unfortunate in terms of element luck, facing very bad life force and spirit essence. This can cause a sudden lack of confidence in one's own abilities and make these two signs prone to being easily discouraged. What the Rat and Boar need this year are strong cures to lift their inner energies. They need to carry the **Life Force Amulet** and **"Om" Dakini Spirit Enhancing Amulet**. What these two signs do have however are a shared *Big Auspicious Star*. Rat and Boar working together can produce very favourable results, and their affinity with each other gets enhanced this year. These two signs will make good business partners. Of the two, Rat will be luckier than Boar, and should take the lead in any endeavor they embark on together.

The EARTH SIGNS of **OX**, **DOG**, **DRAGON** and **SHEEP** all have good life force but bad spirit essence. This suggests that for these signs, they have decent inherent energy, but exposure to the wrong company could be harmful to their mindsets and their motivation levels. They are spiritually weaker than usual and need to carry the **"Om" Dakini Spirit Enhancing Amulet**. Those who are spiritual in nature can draw strength from their belief systems and find solace and comfort in their spiritual practice.

The **SHEEP** meanwhile is also in direct clash with the TAI SUI of the year, and hence the priority for this sign should be to take all steps to appease the God of the Year. The Sheep needs the **Tai Sui Amulet**, and its celestial guardian animal this year should be the **Dragon**

Tai Sui Amulet

Pi Yao. The Sheep can lean on its special friend the Horse, who enjoys superlative luck in 2021. The Sheep working or hanging out with a Horse in the coming year will benefit tremendously from its astrological soulmate. But all four Earth signs are in direct or indirect conflict with the Year God and should thus ALL carry the **Tai Sui Amulet** and have his plaque in the home.

WEALTH LUCK IN 2021

Wealth luck this coming year is weak. It will be difficult to make quick money. Wealth that gets created will come from hard work rather than speculative gains. The year continues to see much disruption to the way business is done, making things difficult for those in sunset industries. Individuals who can spot new opportunities can profit, but increasingly, the free flow of information will reduce the time window for monopolies in new industries. It will be creativity and originality, together with consistent hard work that will allow individuals and businesses to generate income in 2021.

As machines take over more and more jobs, those who do not do something and stubbornly hang on to an old way of life could quickly find themselves being made redundant. The year will not be an easy one for wealth creation, and macro level events continue to depress the immediate outlook.

Certain animal signs will have element luck in their favour when it comes to wealth luck this year; even so, the advice is to weigh all decisions carefully before making them. This is a year when one can take risks, but do not put all your eggs in one basket. Make sure any risks taken are calculated ones backed by understanding and research.

WEALTH ENHANCER: All individuals benefit from inviting in wealth enhancers, particularly the **Asset Wealth Bull** which boosts money and income luck, but also protects against your assets losing value. Those invested in the stock market would benefit greatly from the presence of this bull in the home. It has been designed to look like the stock market bull on Wall Street and carries the meaning "May the market bull for you"; it also features auspicious symbols of good fortune, a red saddle to represent prosperity in 2021, and it is shown presiding over a pile of coins and ingots, signifying its control and dominance over cash. With this bull, you will always have enough money, and even those who sustain losses will quickly make it back.

Asset Wealth Bull

GETTING YOUR TIMING RIGHT:
The Boar in 2021 benefits from carrying the
"Black Tortoise" Constellation Lucky Charms.
Featuring the 7 Sky Animals from the Tortoise
Constellation of the Lunar Mansions, it generates
all the positive attributes of the Tortoise –
support, endurance, longevity and good health.
This will help make up for the weak showing in
the Boar sign's element luck this year. Keeping
these charms close will also help you to get your
timing right when making important decisions
and when acting on them.

"Black Tortoise" Constellation Lucky Charms

LOVE LUCK IN 2021
SINGLES CAN FIND LOVE IN 2021

For singles, this is a promising year for romance. The
Peach Blossom Star has settled into the East, a WOOD
sector, which gives it strength. The East is also the
palace of the Rabbit, which is associated with the
Moon and Moon Goddess who presides over fortunes
related to love and romance. She bestows wishes to

do with relationships, aids in matchmaking soulmates, and improves relations between married couples.

In 2021, the East becomes the place of the "Moon Rabbit" and enhancing this sector manifests love and romance for those looking for true love in their lives. Those wishing to settle down and get married, or searching for their soulmate or one true love, displaying the **Rabbit in the Moon** in the East will manifest this kind of luck for you.

MARRIED COUPLES BEWARE!!!

While there will be plenty of love and romance in 2021, it will not always be the kind that brings happiness. The year's chart also features the *Flower of Romance Star*. Unfortunately, it is the "external" version of this star – making all marriages vulnerable as there will be too much temptation from outside. Innocent flirtations can get out of hand, after-work drinks with colleagues or out-of-town business conferences can lead to inappropriate entanglements, spouses with the seven-year itch could be tempted to act on it. This is a year when those who are married should pay more attention to their other halves.

The *External Star of Romance* often affect those who have grown to take their marriage for granted. As long as you realise it, you can start taking measures to make things right. But what if an affair has already started?

CURE: We advise that when this troublesome star is present, married couples should make

an effort to display symbols of marital stability and happiness in the home. All married couples should have the **Marriage Happiness Ducks** in the home, in the SW, East or center. Each can also carry the **Enhancing Relationships Amulet** to protect against third parties elbowing their way in and "crowding" the marriage.

Displaying the **"Rabbit in the Moon" Love Enhancer** in the home is also an excellent protective measure against stars that affect marital peace and happiness. In 2021, all couples can safeguard their marriage by displaying the Moon Rabbit with the full moon in the East part of their home. For those who suspect their spouse is already cheating, you can call on the help of **Kurukulle**, the powerful Goddess of Love. Invoking her presence in your life imbues you with her

Kurukulle's
Banner of Love

talent for enchantment, giving you your power back when it comes to your spouse and your marriage. You can display her **Banner of Love** or the **Red Tara Home Protection Amulet** – this powerful talisman designed with her image and all her implements of love will repair damage already done to your marriage, while strengthening the bond between you and your spouse.

Kurukulle's powers of magnetism will also make it difficult for others to adversely affect your marriage.

We also advise chanting her mantra daily:
OM KURUKULLE HRIH SOHA (21 times or 108 times)

STUDY LUCK IN 2021

To enhance study luck in 2021, students should call on the help of **Manjushri**, the Buddha of Wisdom. Manjushri with his wisdom sword slices through all ignorance in the mind, enhancing one's wisdom and knowledge. Invoking his help benefits not just students and those studying for exams, but also anyone needing to make important decisions and life choices. He clears the mind to make way for effective and efficient accumulation of knowledge – so that "your knowledge is vast, and your understanding complete". This year we have designed a **Manjushri Home Amulet** for scholars and students to place on their study desk. Manjushri's seed syllable is "DHIH" and chanting this repeatedly in one breath until you run out of breath is the best way to invoke his presence.

You can also chant Manjushri's wisdom mantra:
OM AH RAPA CHA NA DHIH

Make it a habit to chant his mantra either 21 times
or 108 times (1 mala) before you sleep each night, or
when you can find some quiet time during the day. We
suggest you get yourself a **Manjushri Wisdom Mala**
which you reserve specially for this purpose – chanting
only Manjushri's Wisdom Mantra. This sharpens the
mala's power and effectiveness when it comes to study
luck, as the energies you direct into the mala as you
chant becomes concentrated, making it more and more
potent the more you use it.

HEALTH LUCK IN 2021

The Illness Star has flown into the North, the sector of
the Rat. This affects all those born in Rat years, but also
those whose main doors or bedrooms are located in the
North of the home, or those who spend a lot of time in
the North sector. Those afflicted with sickness or health
problems should have the **Healing Deer** in the North.

Health risks continue to look like a threat going into
2021 so we have designed several potent health and
protective talismans to keep everyone safe.

Our **mantra ring** this year features Medicine Buddha's
mantra on the outside and
Vairocana's mantra on the inside.
Medicine Buddha comes to the aid
of anyone who is sick and who
calls to him for help. Vairocana is
the Buddha that protects against

Medicine Buddha-
Vairocana Mantra
Ring

contagious diseases. COVID-19 has been a life-altering phenomenon for the whole world throughout the last year, and as we move into 2021, it does not look like things will revert quite back to normal. We need to continue to practise vigilance following new guidelines as they get discovered to keep safe. Mask up, keep your social distance and get used to a new way of living.

The science of feng shui meanwhile always advocates protection before enhancement, so we strongly advise everyone irrespective of their animal sign to always wear or carry health and protective amulets. It can literally save your life!

The **Medicine Buddha-Vairocana Mantra Ring** is excellent to help keep you safe during these strange and troubled times.

This year we also strongly recommend the **Health Talisman with Tortoise and Snake**. The Tortoise and Snake are two spiritual creatures associated with longevity, known for their potent powers to heal. The tortoise provides stability both in physical and mental health, while the Snake represents control over the nagas, spirits that can cause ill health and sickness when they are left to their own mischievous devices.

All signs whose element luck tables indicate a poor health category should also place these health cures near to them or carry as portable amulets.

Element Luck of the Boar in 2021

Chapter 2

- Fire Boar – 14 & 74 years
- Wood Boar – 26 & 86 years
- Water Boar – 38 years
- Metal Boar – 50 years
- Earth Boar – 62 years

ELEMENT LUCK OF THE BOAR IN 2021

The Boar's element luck chart for 2021 looks unhelpful. For all Boars, your life force, spirit essence and success categories are at very low levels. For some of you, you have better showings in your health and wealth categories, but others will have to ride out the year with low levels here as well. This does not spell all doom and gloom for those born under the Boar sign, as you do have more promising indications from your 24 Mountains chart but it will by no means be an "easy" year.

What will make 2021 better for the Boar is your very excellent attitude towards life! Boars are the optimists of the Chinese Zodiac. You are experts at enjoying life whatever it may throw at you. And when the going is good and you have sufficient inflow of wealth, you know how to enjoy that wealth. When money is tight, you find other ways to stay sufficient, fulfilled and happy.

While the Boar may appear an extravagant spender during more profitable economic times, they are equally good at tightening the belt when circumstances require it of them; all the while without losing their positive outlook and disposition. So if there was ever a sign that could weather a downturn with grace and optimism, it would be the Boar.

ELEMENT LUCK OF

	WOOD BOAR 86/26 years	FIRE BOAR 74/14 years	EARTH BOAR 62/2 years
Life Force	very bad xx	very bad xx	very bad xx
Health	neutral ox	good o	very good oo
Wealth	very bad xx	very good oo	neutral ox
Success	very bad xx	very bad xx	very bad xx
Spirit Essence	very bad xx	very bad xx	very bad xx

THE BOAR IN 2021

METAL BOAR 50 years	WATER BOAR 38 years	2021 Element
very bad xx	very bad xx	Earth
excellent ~~GGG~~	very bad xx	Earth
bad x	**excellent** ~~GGG~~	Metal
very bad xx	very bad xx	Water
very bad xx	very bad xx	Fire

2021 does not look like a year when things come easy, nor is it a year when wealth and profitability will be anything to shout about. But while the charts suggest that this is the case for the Boar, a lot of people this year will be in the same boat. The Boar however has the advantage of being adaptable, constructive and creative in looking for solutions for whatever glitches lie ahead.

This year it is important for the Boar to apply element therapy in their living spaces so your surroundings give you all the help you need to make up for the shortfall brought by an otherwise somewhat discouraging chart.

Your Life Force and Spirit Essence are two areas you need to put special focus on, as these are what will give you the impetus to keep going when the going gets tough, and also what will grant you the strength to get through the trials and tribulations you may have to face in the coming year. To boost your life force, you need Metal element energy; and to boost your inner essence, you need Earth energy. Wearing gemstones set in precious metal with auspicious symbolism will improve these two important categories of luck for you in 2021.

Boars who have Double Happiness Occasions during the year – *hei see* in the form of a big birthday celebration, a new child in the family, or a wedding

– will also successfully counter much of the element shortfall in their luck charts. This makes it a good year to find reasons to celebrate and to throw a big party. Or to get pregnant!

You should also make a conscious effort to be happy and upbeat as much as you can, because when your spirits are high and your mindset is positive, it becomes so much easier to find your way out of the woods.

The Boar is a sociable creature and often draws strength and inspiration from good company - so hang out with friends, continue to socialise, surround yourself with positive people who make you laugh and who make you feel good about things. The worse thing a Boar can do when feeling down is to retreat into his or herself; no Boar person does well alone, as you are naturally social animal. When feeling bad about something, the best solution for you would be to talk it out, or to just "be" with other people so you can take your mind off whatever is getting you down.

For the Boar in 2021, having good friends to turn to or just to hang out with will help very much in improving your mindset and mental health.

All Boars in 2021 need the **Life Force Amulet** and **"Om" Dakini Spirit Enhancing Amulet**. When you lift these two categories of your luck, you automatically put yourself on better footing to get yourself off the ground and back on track with your personal aims and goals. The biggest danger this year for the Boar will not be anything that happens to you externally, but what is going on inside your head. Don't let isolated incidences that mean little become a bone of contention or a reason to get you down. Develop a thicker skin. Don't take things to heart!

Whenever you face a disappointment or failure, remember that it can be used as can be an opportunity to learn, or to give up. Try to ensure it is the former.

Boars are an exceptionally blessed sign of the Zodiac because they usually want for nothing. Boars are born to have very comfortable lives, so it does not take much to make you happy and content. You adjust your life expectations to your personal situation because you are not one to put ambition over your own happiness. The more motivated among you will find a way to balance your ambitions with a healthy social and home life.

Boars tend to be homebodies, enjoying nothing better than playing house. In last year's unprecedented global lockdown, Boars will have been among those who adjusted best and quickest to the "new reality", embracing social means to keep in touch, while hunkering down to ride out the various protocols put in place by governments round the world.

This year will continue to ask more of the same from the Boar. Most of us will not be out of the COVID-19 shadow quite yet, but the Boar sign has the resilience to cope in situations just like these. You adjust your mindset, look for the positives, and keep going!

Success luck is another aspect that needs a boost. Your *lung ta* levels are very low and this calls for the need for the Windhorse. Display the **Victorious Windhorse Carrying a Jewel** in your living and work space to significantly enhance your success potential. Make a conscious decision to enjoy your successes along the way, no matter how small; this will help you stay on track to finish whatever your start.

While this may not be a year to strive for overly lofty goals or grandiose ambitions, you can work on getting a step closer to these goals. But unfortunately the Boar is rarely a longsighted creature. If you don't attain what you consider success immediately, you have the tendency to lose hope or interest, and throw in the towel. The advice is, please don't! Keep going! Because you have two Auspicious Stars helping you – you have a *Big Auspicious* coming from the direction of your Water element friend the Rat, and a *Small Auspicious* from the direction of your sector mate the Dog.

The Boar benefits from hanging in there in 2021. Don't let a lack of immediate success discourage you. Good things come to those who stubbornly stay the course.

WEALTH LUCK
FOR THE DIFFERENT BOARS

Wealth luck differs for the different element Boars, but especially benefits the **38-year-old Water Boar** in 2021. This Boar enjoys excellent element wealth luck, which suggests that financially, this Boar will be secure, and its wealth can grow. The **74-year-old Fire Boar** also has very good element wealth luck. To take full advantage, this Boar should display the **Tree Bringing 3 Kinds of Wealth** in its living space; this will add growth energy to its wealth potential, boosting career and investment luck, and for some, even attract a windfall.

The **62-year-old Earth Boar** has neutral element wealth luck, suggesting that while you could be doing better financially, you are not in trouble. Even if cash flow becomes tight, you find a way to cope.

The **50-year-old Metal Boar** has a less robust indication in your wealth category. The advice for this

Boar is to steer clear of risky investments. For you, the best strategy is to maintain a sufficiently diversified portfolio. Do not succumb to taking financial risks, no matter how irresistible, as luck is not with you when it comes to money matters in 2021.

The **26-year-old** and **86-year-old Wood Boars** have their wealth category at a VERY BAD level, so this is a warning to take serious steps to preserve wealth this year! Avoid taking risks when it comes to money. This is not a year for frivolous expenditures. Unexpected expenses could crop up, disrupting your personal financial plan for the year. Be conservative, do not spend in excess, and limit your exuberance when it comes to spending money. This Boar needs the **"Hum" Dakini Wealth Protection Amulet** to safeguard their wealth.

HEALTH OF THE BOAR

The only Boar with anything serious to worry about when it comes to health is the **38-year-old Water Boar**. For this Boar, you should pay more attention to your physical well-being. Go for regular check-ups. If you don't feel well for any reason, get it looked at. Do not leave health concerns to a point when it is too late to do anything about it. While you may be active and feeling fit as a fiddle, never take your health for granted, especially this year!

This Boar should carry the **Health Talisman Holder with Health Mantras** and have the **Medicine Buddha & the 7 Sugatas Gau** near you. Be mindful not to expose yourself to infectious viruses; post COVID19, you must absolutely not take any risks when it comes to contagious diseases. If there are quarantine recommendations in place, follow them! Don't be foolhardy and think you are invincible, because this year, health-wise, you are far from it.

FIRE BOAR 14 year old	
life force	very bad xx
health	good o
wealth	very good oo
success	very bad xx
spirit essence	very bad xx

THE 14-YEAR-OLD FIRE BOAR

Of the Boars, this young Fire Boar has the most promising element luck chart in 2021. This Boar has good levels of health luck, and wealth is also extremely promising. At your young age, wealth is not an aspiration that is especially important to you, as you are not yet of working age. But having good wealth luck means you will not be short of money. You have the funds you need to study, to continue your various co-curricular activities and for all the creature comforts you may need or have become accustomed to.

The young Boar is often incredibly delightful, and the easy favourite within family circles. Your parents love you, you are the darling or all the aunts and uncles, and you are likely very popular at school. Boars make natural teacher's pets if they choose to be. You are responsible, compassionate and empathetic with others, and you get along as well with adults as with other children your own age.

The coming year may not be as smooth-going as some others, because you have weak element luck in three categories; but you can nevertheless make good progress. Think of 2021 as a foundation year, one in which you build a solid grounding for future success. When you study, do a thorough job so you are on firm footing as you advance in your course.

In your other activities, pick one you particularly enjoy, and give yourself a goal to really master it. Your strong health and wealth luck are indications that with the willpower and right attitude, you can easily overcome the less favourable elements in your chart to make 2021 a year to remember.

This Boar benefits from the **Manjushri "Dhih" Scholastic Amulet** - clip onto your schoolbag. For scholastic luck and exam success, place **Manjushri's Gau** on your study desk. Manjushri is the Buddha of

Manjushri "Dhih"
Scholastic Amulet

Wisdom who will help you achieve significant success in your studies.

WOOD BOAR 26 year old	
life force	very bad *xx*
health	neutral *ox*
wealth	very bad *xx*
success	very bad *xx*
spirit essence	very bad *xx*

THE 26-YEAR-OLD WOOD BOAR

The **26-year-old Wood Boar** does not have good element luck in 2021. All your categories of luck are unfortunately negative, with only your health category registering a neutral reading. This suggests that this is a year to stay quiet and lie low. Avoid making changes in your life that may be risky. If you have a current job, best to keep it for now; finding another one will not be so easy. Be thankful for what you have and stop coveting the greener grass on the other side of the fence.

Those just finishing their studies and entering the job market will not be able to be so picky when it comes to which job offer to accept. Even if you may not get your dream job immediately, make the most of what you get, because luck for you comes in unexpected ways and from unexpected sources this year. There is definitely hidden luck to be tapped, but you mustn't be impatient.

Wealth luck is very bad, so beware investing your own money in risky ventures. If choosing between getting a job or branching out on your own, better go with the safer option. Focus on building your skills, experience and connections for the future. A good year for laying ground work and establishing a strong network.

This Boar needs to carry the **Life Force Amulet** and the **"Om" Dakini Spirit Enhancing Amulet**.

WATER BOAR 38 year old	
life force	very bad xx
health	very bad xx
wealth	excellent ooo
success	very bad xx
spirit essence	very bad xx

THE 38-YEAR-OLD WATER BOAR

The **38-year-old Water Boar** enjoys excellent wealth luck, but very poor luck in all other categories. Your life force, spirit essence, success and health categories are extremely weak, so you need to exercise caution this year. Do not take your health for granted, and do not let yourself become overcome by stress. Don't put off a trip to the doctor's. Seek professional medical advice if you think you need it. When it comes to your health, better be safe than sorry. Don't leave it till it becomes too late to do anything. Health is not something you can take for granted this year.

Devise a healthy lifestyle for yourself. Make time for regular exercise. Eat sensibly and get enough rest. Those working in stressful jobs should find a way to periodically switch off to take your mind off things. It is important to de-stress, especially if you start to find that a lot of your waking moments are stressful ones.

If you don't have a hobby, this may be the time to explore developing one. It would benefit you a lot to have something to take your mind somewhere else and to engage you in different ways. It will also enlarge your circle of friends and bring you into contact with fresh new ideas. This year, work at expanding the horizons in your life a little more.

This Boar benefits from health enhancers. Carry the **Health Talisman Holder** with health mantras or the **Medicine Buddha Amulet** for good health. You can also keep **Medicine Buddha's Mantra Wand** near you. This will help you guard against illness. If you are already suffering from ill health of any kind, it will help you recover. For money luck, this Boar should display the **Ox Finding Hidden Wealth** in the West of your living or work room.

Ox Finding Hidden Wealth

METAL BOAR 50 year old	
life force	very bad xx
health	excellent ooo
wealth	bad x
success	very bad xx
spirit essence	very bad xx

THE 50-YEAR-OLD METAL BOAR

The **50-year-old Metal Boar** enjoys excellent health luck this year. This is a great indication as it suggests you have the energy to take on anything you wish to. Whether your goals are physical, intellectual or monetary in nature, you have the energy to go after them. You are operating at a good level of productivity, and are as robust physically as you are mentally.

But wealth luck is not promising, so while you can make some progress this year, your wealth goals may fall short. This is not a year to take big financial risks. When it comes to money, this Boar should stay conservative.

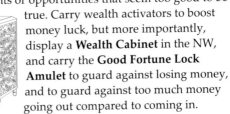

Have enough in the bank for a rainy day. Be wary of investments or opportunities that seem too good to be

true. Carry wealth activators to boost money luck, but more importantly, display a **Wealth Cabinet** in the NW, and carry the **Good Fortune Lock Amulet** to guard against losing money, and to guard against too much money going out compared to coming in.

Wealth Cabinet

Turn your focus towards non-monetary goals. Big financial success is likely to elude you, and those who have your own money at stake could get very streesed out. Do not gamble and avoid speculation. The only way for this Boar to make money this year is through old-fashioned hard work. Don't be too hard on yourself if you don't achieve the results you are looking for. Your wealth luck is nothing to shout about this year, so draw satisfaction from other aspects of your life.

As well as displaying wealth cabinets, this Boar can carry the **Income Generating Amulet** to boost your weak wealth luck this year.

Income Generating Amulet

EARTH BOAR 62 year old	
life force	very bad xx
health	very good GG
wealth	neutral Gx
success	very bad xx
spirit essence	very bad xx

THE 62-YEAR-OLD EARTH BOAR

This Boar can look forward to a moderate year. Your health luck is looking good, which gives you the energy to stay busy and active. But your wealth luck is merely neutral, which suggests that while there is money to be made, it is unlikely to be big money. You will be financially secure but should work at deriving happiness not from how well you are doing financially but from other things, as money will not be your strong suit in 2021.

The Earth Boar is a homebody at heart, and while those working or in business will be devoted to what you do, this year gives you the opportunity to turn your sights to other things as well. Direct more attention towards your family and enjoying what the fruits of your labour over the past years can buy. This year you can step back from such a hectic workload and let your business run itself. Allow your deputies to do more. You don't need to be the one making every decision. Forget the one-man show deal – you benefit from help, and from having assistants and collaborators.

Your good health reading however indicates that you have plenty of energy to devote to things that interest you. This may be a year then to discover new interests and hobbies, perhaps even something that lets you change professional direction! Some of you may have reached a plateau in your professional work. If the excitement is no longer there, this is an opportune year to actively seek new challenges. Or bring fresh new ideas to your current table.

Those with children and even grandchildren can derive much pleasure from playing the grand old patriarch or matriarch, or grandpa or nana. Spend time nurturing the family and simply enjoying them. The world is changing so quickly and the best way to keep up is to mix with the younger generations. For the Boar, there's no better place to turn to than to your own family!

This Boar benefits from the **Vase with Bats of Abundance**. You should focus on abundance in your life in the broadest sense. This vase attracts good fortune luck in the form of prosperity but also in the quality of your relationships with each other. It ensures you can continue your abundant lifestyle and enjoy it with your family.

FIRE BOAR 74 year old	
life force	very bad xx
health	good o
wealth	very good oo
success	very bad xx
spirit essence	very bad xx

THE 74-YEAR-OLD FIRE BOAR

The **74-year-old Fire Boar** can look forward to a year of good health luck and very good wealth luck, so there is little standing in your way to making this a very pleasant time ahead. The Fire Boar is the most intense amongst all your Boar siblings, and you feel everything more deeply.

You are also the most ambitious of the 5 Boars. You are endlessly optimistic and rarely allow yourself to get perturbed by temporary blips and obstacles.

The coming year has promising indications, and with your inborn optimism, you are able to spot those opportunities, even if they may be obscured by minor disappointments along the way. How big your problems are will depend only on your own mindset towards them. Actively draw on your natural laissez-faire attitude to go with the flow. Don't let anything worry or upset you. This is the best way for this Boar to get the most out of the year.

Do not fear the unknown. If there is something you've always wanted to do, make plans to do it! Take up a new hobby, learn a new skill, make some new friends. Be bold and brave! Lots of new delights await those who are prepared to jump in with no reservations or preconceptions!

This Boar should display the **God of Longevity** in your living space. He will help ensure you age gracefully and brings the blessings of a long life free of health woes or financial anxiety. You also benefit from **Vajrasattva's Mantra Wand**. Vajrasattva purifies all negativities in your life, removing obstacles to happiness and good luck.

God of Longevity

Four Pillars Chart
2021
Chapter 3

FOUR PILLARS CHART 2021

An important indicator of the potential of any year is the Four Pillars chart of the year. This reveals the impact of the five elements of the year. When all five elements are present, it indicates a balance, a preferred situation. In feng shui, we are always striving for balance, and when something is out of balance, we always endeavor to bring things back into balance by introducing the missing element. This year, the chart

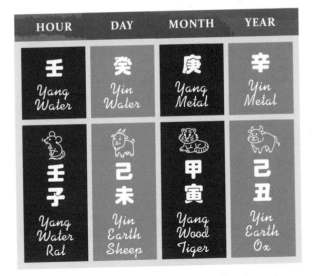

HOUR	DAY	MONTH	YEAR
壬	癸	庚	辛
Yang Water	Yin Water	Yang Metal	Yin Metal
壬子	己未	甲寅	己丑
Yang Water Rat	Yin Earth Sheep	Yang Wood Tiger	Yin Earth Ox

This year's Four Pillars charts lacks Fire, the element that signifies wealth luck.

is obviously missing Fire, the element that indicates WEALTH LUCK, so the year lacks opportunities to make money.

However, the eight characters in the Four Pillars – made up of 4 heavenly stems and 4 earthly branches – are not the only elements present. The interaction of these elements, depending on where and how they are positioned within the chart, generates a set of hidden elements as well as special stars. We use this chapter to analyse each part of this year's Four Pillars chart, and mention the most significant findings.

2021's Paht Chee chart indicates a strong self-element of Water, which boosts competitive energies and puts everyone on edge. Friends become foes when the stakes are raised, so this is a year to constantly watch one's back. The year's chart is unbalanced; it is missing the vital element of FIRE, which represents wealth and financial success. It is thus a year when it will be difficult to make much headway in the creation of new wealth. Profits may take a long time to get realized and there are few speculative gains to be made.

Prosperity comes with hard work rather than with a stroke of luck. This is definitely not a year to strike it rich via the lottery.

Here is a closer look at the most important indications this year:

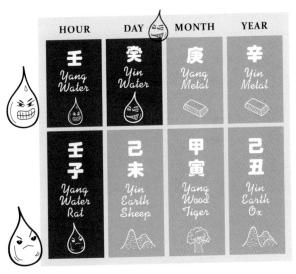

HOUR	DAY	MONTH	YEAR
壬 Yang Water	癸 Yin Water	庚 Yang Metal	辛 Yin Metal
壬子 Yang Water Rat	己未 Yin Earth Sheep	甲寅 Yang Wood Tiger	己丑 Yin Earth Ox

There appears to be way too much Water in this year's chart.

A YEAR OF STRONG WATER
indicating a competitive year

First, the self-element of the year is Strong Water. It is a year when rivalry becomes enhanced and when politics can get unscrupulous. Watch your back and reserve your trust for your very innermost circle. Indeed, even your inner circle could let you down if the circumstances dictate. Betrayals happen of their own accord, sometimes without the guilty party's conscious intention. Learn to forgive and move on but protect yourself by being more careful and by putting safeguards in place. Remove temptation where you can and stay close to all you are working with.

 PROTECTION: Those in business are advised to carry the **Kuan Kung on Horseback Anti-Betrayal Amulet**. This will protect you against the betrayal of others and being let down by people whom you trust. It keeps you prepared for whatever the winds and waters bring your way.

In any competitive endeavour, it could well feel like a fight to the death. Diplomatic compromises will be difficult to achieve, and different factions and interest groups find it harder to reach win-win scenarios. But it is nevertheless important to try. Sometimes being the bigger person will help; but recognize when you have to fight and when you don't. Indeed, do not mistakenly think you are in fact being the magnanimous one when you are being taken for a fool. It is a year when it is prudent to carry protection always. The **28 Hums Protection Amulet** is an excellent all-round amulet that will safeguard you from all kinds of harm.

SOLUTION: The excess of Water energy in the chart needs to be resolved. Use **WOOD energy** to weaken the excess Water. Having plenty of greenery and live plants in your living space will help re-balance the energies and will also bring vital growth energy to a year which lacks the presence of the *Lap Chun*, or "Spring".

This year, having plenty of plants and Wood energy in the home will help soak up the excess Water in the years chart.

BALANCE OF YIN & YANG

Second, there are two Yang pillars and two Yin Pillars. There is thus a good mix between energetic periods and restive ones, with no dominance of work over play, or vice versa. The Yang Month and Hour Pillars bring great vitality, while the Yin Year and Day Pillars bring balance. There should be more than enough strength to propel positive chi forward and upward. People in general are open to different viewpoints. If negative energies can be kept under control and sufficiently subdued, the year is then able to propel forward, benefitting many.

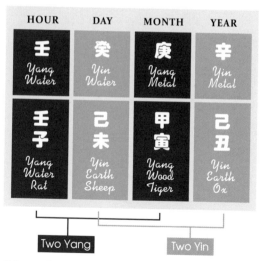

This year there is good balance between Yang and Yin in the years Four Pillars chart.

CLASH OF SHEEP WITH OX
indicating strong conflict energy

Third, there is a clash of SHEEP with OX in the Earth Branches. This clash between two Earth animals suggests that the clash will be between leaders. Earth is the element that represents leadership and rank, thus animosity will likely be between those who are in charge. But because those in power are especially strong this year, fighting can become ferocious, with the damage dealt far-reaching. There will be strong clashes between the leaders of nations.

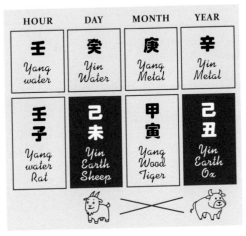

HOUR	DAY	MONTH	YEAR
壬	癸	庚	辛
Yang water	Yin Water	Yang Metal	Yin Metal
壬子	己未	甲寅	己丑
Yang water Rat	Yin Earth Sheep	Yang Wood Tiger	Yin Earth Ox

The clash between Ox and Sheep brings many problems to the year, especially between those who are in charge, and everyone else could end up as collateral damage.

Within family units, because the clash occurs in the Day Pillar, there is likely to be strong conflict between spouses.

SOLUTION: There may be more marital problems in 2021 with the Sheep in the Self-Spouse pillar clashing with the Year pillar. In the family unit, this coupled with the presence of the *External Flower of Romance* star brings all kinds of problems to husband and wife. Every home this year should have the **"Rabbit in the Moon" Love Enhancer** and better still if both husband and wife carry the **Enhancing Relationships Amulet**. Recognize when an outsider is trying to make trouble in your marriage, and refrain from siding with a third party over your spouse, no matter how much your husband or wife may be annoying you. When you allow an outsider into the mix, this year, such troubles can escalate very quickly.

Enhancing Relationships Amulet

SPECIAL LINK BETWEEN RAT & OX
bringing creativity and inventiveness

Fourth, there is however a very strong affinity between RAT and OX in the Earthly Branches of the Year and Hour Pillar. This is a heaven sent because it serves to repair some of the damage resulting from the Ox-Sheep clash. The Year Pillar of the Ox forms a soulmate pairing with the Hour Pillar of the Rat, which means there is a good beginning and a good ending to the year, what the Chinese refer to as having a head and tail, a suggestion that things that

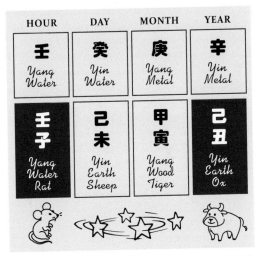

HOUR	DAY	MONTH	YEAR
壬 Yang Water	癸 Yin Water	庚 Yang Metal	辛 Yin Metal
壬子 Yang Water Rat	己未 Yin Earth Sheep	甲寅 Yang Wood Tiger	己丑 Yin Earth Ox

The Rat and Ox in this year's chart forms a very special affinity, bringing relationship and completion luck.

get started have a good chance to reach satisfactory completion. The two signs of Rat and Ox are extremely harmonious together, generating the *House of Cleverness and Creativity*, with the Rat starting and the Ox completing. This endows the year with wonderful ingenuity and inventiveness.

The presence of the Rat & Ox in the year's Four Pillars suggests a year when true friendship means something.

These two signs are also a secret-friend pair, indicating **good friendship luck** through the year. While there are indications of strong competition and rivalry, there is also much potential for firm friendships, and opportunities for friends to demonstrate their loyalties and allegiance. A year perhaps of finding out who one's true friends are.

ENHANCER: Get the **"Perfect Partnerships to Attract Big Wealth" Enhancer**. This enhancer featuring the Ox and Rat will boost all the positive indications of this combination. Display in a prominent area in the home; in the living room, or near the dining room where you spend a lot of time. The number "8" on the Ox activates for the missing wealth luck of the year.

NO PROSPERITY LUCK INDICATED
... *but there is hidden wealth*

Fifth, there is MISSING WEALTH. Fire which represents wealth is completely missing from the main chart. What this indicates is that it will be difficult to make money. New businesses will take time getting off the ground, sales will be slow, industries that are shrinking will continue to do so, while their replacements will take time to take flight. Profit margins get squeezed as information becomes more and more freely available, and technology continues to disrupt at breakneck pace. This year, if one wants to stay afloat, it is vitally important to keep up with the world that is so rapidly changing around us.

While there will be results and completions, it will nevertheless feel like an interim year, because we are at the beginning end of a new cycle, and not quite at the close of the current period. 2021 represents the second animal sign of the cycle after the new decade last year opened with the Rat, and we are heading towards the end of Period 8, and the beginning of Period 9, but we are not quite there yet.

There is a lack of obvious wealth in 2021, but those who look harder can find gold. This year, there is HIDDEN WEALTH brought by the sign of the TIGER.

While WEALTH luck may be lacking, there is however HIDDEN WEALTH brought by the TIGER. This will bring some respite, and keep us tided over, but it is wealth that comes in its own time rather than overnight. What this means is that 2021 is a year when we can lay the foundations for future wealth, but we must not get our hopes up for immediate results.

That the hidden wealth star is brought by the Tiger bodes well for friends of the Tiger – the Dog and especially the Horse.

The Dog enjoys one *Small Auspicious Star* from the 24 mountains chart, while the Horse enjoys not one but *TWO Big Auspicious Stars*, together with a *Golden Deity Star*. These two astrological allies of the big cat are lucky in this respect in terms of money-making prospects, although all signs can boost wealth luck with suitable activators and enhancers.

THE COLOUR FOR WEALTH: The wearing of the most auspicious colour of the spectrum RED will bring significant added benefits in 2021. Red is the colour which represents ultimate YANG, which serves to boost the year's vitality, but will do double duty in enhancing the missing Wealth element of the year. Red in 2021 stands for WEALTH, so wearing this colour as part of your wardrobe or accessories will give you a boost of good fortune. You should also carry the **"Increase Your Wealth Luck" Gold Talisman Card** featuring the God of Wealth Tsai Shen Yeh

seated on a Tiger. This will attract wealth of the kind that keeps increasing and will help you tap the hidden wealth luck of the year.

You can also display the **Bejewelled God of Wealth sitting on a Tiger** in figurine form in the home.

Bejewelled God of Wealth sitting on a Tiger

Before the New Year arrives, make sure you get our specially created **Red Wealth Wallet** featuring the Wealth Ox. It is auspicious each year to change to a new wallet and especially lucky to take some money from your old wallet and transfer it over to your new wallet. Doing so for this year will ensure you take some of the energy of last year, and carry it over into the following year. In 2021 you definitely want to do this, as the previous Year of the Rat carried two *Lap Chuns*, or two "Springs" while this year has none.

Keep the lights in your home brightly turned on throughout the year, especially in the WEST sector, which plays host to the Prosperity Star #8.

POWERFUL SPIRITUAL ENHANCER: For Wealth Luck that is potent and long-lasting, an excellent ritual to incorporate into your life is the **White Dzambala Ritual**. Invite in **White Dzambala and the Four Dakinis** who pull in

wealth from the four directions. Display in a respectful place in the home and recite White Dzambala's mantra as regularly as you can.

White Dzambala's Mantra:
*Om Padma Krodha Arya Dzambala
Hridaya Hum Phat*

When you gaze upon him and chant his mantra regularly, he manifests great riches in your life and attracts incredible opportunities that can bring wealth of a big meaningful and lasting kind.

INVITE IN THE ROOSTER: The Rooster brings the #8 Wealth Star in 2021, so it is extremely auspicious to have many images of Roosters in the home this year. The Rooster is also the symbol that ensures politicking is kept to a minimum, protecting against harmful gossip and slander. The Rooster is also wonderful for protecting the marriage, preventing any troublesome third party from trying to come between husband and wife.

Rooster with Crown

There are many benefits to displaying the Rooster this year; indeed, it may be a good time to start collecting Roosters, made of different colours and in different materials if you wish. You can also display Rooster Art in the home, which is most auspicious. Display in the West part of the home.

Our new **Rooster with Crown** this year has been embellished with powerful symbols of protection and good fortune, to ensure the negative energies of the year cannot harm you. It features the "Anti Evil-Eye" to protect against jealousy, the Double Dorje for wisdom in decision making and the powerful "Hum" seed syllable for strong protection. Its powerful feathers sweep away all harmful energies and its crown symbolizes holding dominion over the year.

LUCKY SPECIAL STARS OF 2021

Sixth, there are two potentially VERY AUSPICIOUS stars in the year's Four Pillars chart. These are seriously good stars noted for being strong and very explicit in their beneficial influence. These stars have the capability of bringing incredible good fortune to those who know how to activate them correctly, while making sure the positive aspects of their influences materialize.

These stars impact different animal signs differently and in varying degrees, but are nevertheless very beneficial for all signs. Note that you will need to wear or carry the relevant activators to ensure that you make the most of the positive influence of these stars.

THE STAR OF PROSPECTS
brings many new opportunities

This star brought by the Earthly Branch of Rat in the Hour Pillar with the self-element of Water indicates many new opportunities in the coming year. This favourable star conjures up a very special energy that rewards determination and staying power, resonating

HOUR	DAY	MONTH	YEAR
壬 *Yang Water*	癸 *Yin Water*	庚 *Yang Metal*	辛 *Yin Metal*
壬 子 *Yang Water Rat*	己 未 *Yin Earth Sheep*	甲 寅 *Yang Wood Tiger*	己 丑 *Yin Earth Ox*

The Star of Prospects brings many new opportunities in the coming year.

with the Ox sign of the year, a reminder that those who retain their passion for success will benefit from its presence. This star suggests there is nothing that cannot be achieved for those prepared to work hard. The more ambitious one is, the further one can go this year.

STAR OF PROSPECTS: To activate this star in your favour, keep an **image of an Ox** near you. We suggest the **Bejewelled Asset Bull** to magnify wealth luck and to ensure the hard work you put in meets with proportionate success. This bull has been designed with an auspicious saddle in red, the colour that signifies wealth in 2021, wearing a harness of coins and stepping on a pile of wealth and ingots, symbolizing the accumulation of assets.

This beautiful enhancer will allow you to accumulate everything you work for and ensure you do not spend everything you earn. It will also increase the opportunities that come your way.

THE STAR OF POWERFUL MENTORS
brings Benefactor Luck

The Star of Powerful Mentors which was also in last year's chart makes another appearance in 2021. This star is brought by the OX in the Year Pillar and the Heavenly Stem of YANG METAL in the Month Pillar. This star is especially beneficial for the younger generation, who have the auspicious luck of influential people turning up in their lives to help them, giving them meaningful advice and powerful support.

HOUR	DAY	MONTH	YEAR
壬	癸	庚	辛
Yang Water	Yin Water	Yang Metal	Yin Metal
壬子	己未	甲寅	己丑
Yang Water Rat	Yin Earth Sheep	Yang Wood Tiger	Yin Earth Ox

The Star of Powerful Mentors is particularly beneficial for the younger generation.

For students hungry for success, mentors will open doors to scholarship, and teachers will provide fabulous inspiration and motivation. Opportunities abound and there will be unseen hands supporting you. Those just starting out in your careers can find a mentor figure to guide you and to show you the ropes. An influential boss could fast-track your promotion up the ranks.

ACTIVATE THE STAR OF POWERFUL MENTORS: Bring this star to life by displaying **Kuan Kung** in the home. You can also display near to you work or study desk. Another powerful activator for this star is the **Nobleman Qui Ren Talisman**. The benefits of this special star are immense, so it is worth activating. It brings help from the heavens, manifesting someone in your life with the wish and means to help you, and ensures those with this kind of power stay firmly on your side.

AFFLICTIVE STARS OF 2021

There are two unlucky stars brought by the Four Pillars chart of the year. These, when not attended to with relevant cures, can wreak a lot of havoc and create a lot of misfortune, but their ill influence can be avoided if you take special note and address them.

THE AGGRESSIVE SWORD STAR
is a Double-Edged Sword

The Aggressive Sword Star formed by the Yin Water in the Heavenly Stem of the Day Pillar and the Earthly Branch of Ox in the Year Pillar suggests a year of

HOUR	DAY	MONTH	YEAR
壬 Yang Water	癸 Yin Water	庚 Yang Metal	辛 Yin Metal
壬子 Yang Water Rat	己未 Yin Earth Sheep	甲寅 Yang Wood Tiger	己丑 Yin Earth Ox

The Aggressive Sword Star can be both good or bad.

intense aggression. It indicates the strengthening of the underdog's chi, so it points to a rise of revolutionary fervour, people revolting against authority. Strikes continue, spawning groups around the globe to walk similar paths. Protests advocating for greater equality, non-discrimination, fighting against police brutality and other social injustices continue to pick up steam. There will be anger, passion, rioting and violence.

At its pinnacle, the presence of this star suggests the emergence of powerful leaders on opposing sides, or of highly influential opposition to established leaders. It suggests the rise of a people who seize power by fair means or foul. The name of this star is *Yang Ren*, which describes "*yang essence sharp blade that inflicts damage*". This is a star with great potential for either very good or very bad influences to materialize during the year, although generally, the influence tends to be more negative than positive. There is risk of revolution and of the toppling of unpopular leaders in power.

The Aggressive Sword Star brings potential for violence & bloodshed. This star must be strongly subdued.

In this year's chart, the *Star of Aggressive Sword* is created by the strong YIN WATER of the DAY pillar, with the presence of the OX in the YEAR pillar. Here, note that the WATER element is strong in the chart, making the presence of the Aggressive Sword much more negative. It indicates that those emerging as leaders for the underdog in 2021 will end up being heavy-handed and quick-tempered. They may be charismatic but they will also be strong-willed, conceited, arrogant, overbearing and self-centered - all nasty traits that spell the potential for bloodshed and violence wherever they emerge. There is real danger of that this year!

CURE: To shield against the harmful effects of the Aggressive Sword Star, the best remedy is a powerful spiritual Stupa. The **Kumbum Stupa** is especially beneficial as it contains one hundred holy images, invoking the protection of all the world's Wisdom Protectors. This Stupa will ensure that all family members living within the home stay protected against aggression or violence of any kind. It is also a good idea to wear or carry the **28 Hums Protection Wheel Amulet** at all times.

Kumbum Stupa

THE FLOWER OF ROMANCE STAR (EXTERNAL) *makes marriages vulnerable*

This star is sometimes confused with the *Peach Blossom Star* because it addresses the destiny of love; but while both influence love and romance, they are very different in their effects. When the Flower of Romance is present, it suggests love blossoms easily, but it is not the kind of love that leads to marriage and family. It indicates instead the possibility of extramarital affairs, bringing stress and unhappiness to married couples. There is also a difference between *internal* and *external romance*, and in this year of the Ox, it is unfortunately the latter that prevails. So the year is

HOUR	DAY	MONTH	YEAR
壬 Yang Water	癸 Yin Water	庚 Yang Metal	辛 Yin Metal
壬子 Yang Water Rat	己未 Yin Earth Sheep	甲寅 Yang Wood Tiger	己丑 Yin Earth Ox

The External Flower of Romance Star brings stress and risk of infidelity in marriages.

likely to see increased occurrences of infidelity and break-ups of marriages.

Marriages are vulnerable to the External Flower of Romance this year.

The SHEEP in the Day Pillar and RAT of the Hour Pillar indicate the presence of the *External Romance Star*, making all marriages vulnerable to straying by husband OR wife. Things are made worse as the Sheep clashes with the ruling animal of the year, the Ox. This causes misunderstandings between couples, and danger of an outsider fanning the flames from the side.

FIXING THE EXTERNAL STAR OF ROMANCE: To prevent this affliction from doing real harm to your marriage, carry the **Enhancing Relationships Amulet**, especially if you suspect your spouse already has eyes for someone outside your marriage. Or if you are constantly fighting with each other, or forced into a situation when you have to spend large amounts of time apart (e.g. if one of you commutes to a different country for work, or travel a lot for work). It is also a good idea to display a pair of **Marriage Happiness Ducks** in the SW of the home, or if you suspect something has already started, place an **Amethyst Geode** tied with red string under the foot of the bed of the straying partner.

You can also invite in the **image of an Ox and Horse** to counter the affliction. This subdues the possibility of infidelity causing problems for you. The OX/HORSE presence will create a special "cross" with the SHEEP/RAT affliction.

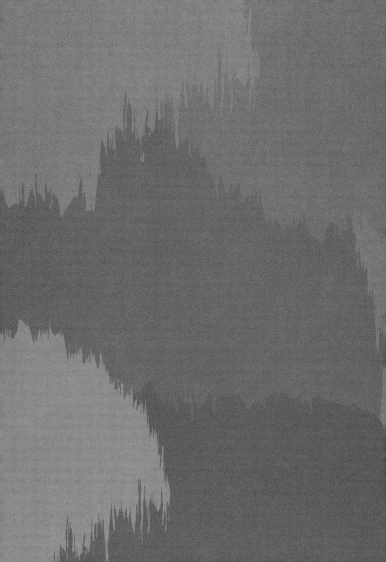

Flying Stars of 2021
Chapter 4

FLYING STAR CHART OF 2021
Heavenly Star *rules the year*

The Flying Star chart on first glance is a big improvement on last year's chart. The Loss Star #7 of 2020 makes way for the *Heaven Star* #6 in this Year of the Ox 2021. The Heaven Star becomes the dominant star of this year. This white star is associated with many good things, attracting the celestial luck of the heavens and providing the unseen hand of opportunity and guidance from above. Everyone stands to benefit from this star, especially if the center of the home where the star is located is kept well-energized and active throughout the year.

In 2021, it benefits to keep the center of the home very active! Have friends over & use this space well.

Rearrange your furniture so you naturally gravitate to the center of your home. The more you include this space in daily usage, the better the luck of the whole family for this coming year.

2021's chart suits homes with open plan layouts arranged around the center part of the home. This is where the luck of auspicious heaven energy congregates this year, and keeping this part of the home lively and vibrant with lots of music, chatter and activity will serve to "activate" this star, bringing it to life!

Work at repositioning your furniture and seating if you have to. This year it is extremely auspicious for all members of the household to spend plenty of time in the center sector, and when you have guests, entertain them in this part of the home. If your home has a piano, place it in the center so every time someone sits down to play it, the sector gets energized.

If your home is not an open-concept one, keep the doors to the center room in the home ajar as much as possible.

You want the energy that emanates from the center to seep into all other areas of the home. The more you energize this part of your house, and the more you suppress the bad luck sectors, the better the luck of the whole household for the year.

ENHANCE THE CENTER GRID
with the Celestial Water Dragon

This year, every household benefits from the presence of the **Celestial Water Dragon**. Place this celestial creature in the center of your home and of your office. The celestial Dragon is the ultimate symbol of good fortune and its deep blue colour and cloud imagery suggest its heavenly origins. This Dragon is auspicious wherever he is displayed, but this year he especially benefits the center part of the home, which houses the Heaven Star #6.

The Celestial Water Dragon is the best enhancer for the #6 Heaven Star which occupies the central sector in 2021.

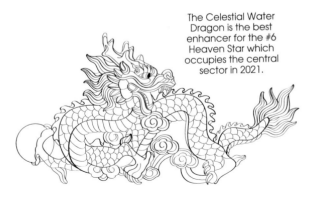

Placing the Celestial Water Dragon here will attract plenty of new and lucrative opportunities into your life, as well as the patrons, mentors and contacts you need to support you in whatever path you choose to take. Individuals and organizations who are in a position to help you and to open doors for you, will somehow find their way into your life. The presence of the celestial Dragon always attracts abundance and success, and this year, inviting in this Dragon brings a very special kind of good fortune indeed.

Invoking the power of
THE EIGHT IMMORTALS

Another excellent energizer for the center is the **8 Celestial Immortals Plaque**. The 8 Immortals bring eight kinds of good fortune and protects against harm. In Chinese mythology, they are a revered group of legendary beings each with a unique talent or ability.

Place the 8 Immortals Plaque in the center of the home in 2021.

These eight saints have been depicted in Chinese art since time immemorial as they are believed to bestow wealth, longevity and spiritual awakening on all who glance upon them.

Depicted as a group, they bring a balanced basket of good fortune and protection for the whole family. They hail from the 8 different compass directions and are usually shown with their unique symbols representing the luck each brings.

Zhang Guo Lao, protector of the North, **brings the luck of good descendants**. His symbol is the bamboo flute and his element is Water. He enjoys drinking wine and is famous for making his own which had curative and healing powers. He is said to be able to drink poison without harm and offers protection against the dark arts. He is often shown with his companion, the mule.

Chao Guo Jiu, protector of the Northeast, **brings the luck of control**. He is excellent for those in positions of authority who have to motivate and retain the support of those they command. His element is Earth and his symbol are the castanets. According to legend, he went to great lengths to avoid casualties of war, protecting the innocent from harm during battle. He is skilled in the magical arts and possesses great wisdom and charisma to lead with great authority.

Lee Dong Bin, protector of the West, **brings protection against evil**. His element is Metal and his implement is the Magic Sword. He is famed for being a great scholar and poet, and for his exceptional intelligence. While he had certain character flaws – he was a serial womanizer - he was known for his dedication to helping others elevate their spiritual growth.

He Xian Gu, protector of the Southwest, **bestows family and marriage luck**. Her element is Earth and her symbol is the Lotus Blossom. The only lady among the 8, she has also grown to become a symbol of woman power. She is often accompanied by a mythical bird said to reign over all birds, bringing new opportunities from near and far. She helps stabilize married couples, protecting the sacred sanctity of marriage and bestowing a happy family life. She protects against troublemakers who threaten to break up happy families. For those who are single, she is said to attract marriage opportunities and suitable suitors.

Han Xiang Zi, protector of the Southeast, **brings healing energies** to those who are sick, but more particularly, he helps heal those with a broken heart. His element is Wood and his symbol is the flute. His legendary past involves the tragic love story where he fell in love with the daughter of the Dragon King, who did not grant the couple his blessings. Theirs was a star-crossed romance without a happy ending, but the bamboo flute he wields was said to be a gift from his beloved. Playing on his flute healed him emotionally, and from there on he vowed to help others the same way.

Lan Chai He, protector of the Northwest, **brings scholastic and creative luck**. His element is Metal and his symbol the flower basket. He is often shown with his swan, symbolic of his lyrical gifts. He is said to have become immortal when the Monkey King bestowed 500 years of magic upon him. His companion is the Monkey. As well as his flair for the arts, he is said to possess a sharp intelligence and wit.

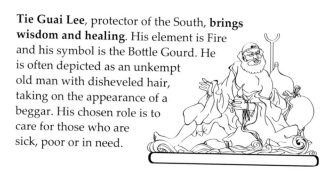

Han Zhong Li, protector of the East, **brings longevity and wealth**. His element is Wood and his symbols are the magical fan and peach. His fan is said to have the ability to heal the sick, even bring the dead back to life, as well as turning stones to silver and gold. His peach is the fruit of immortality which grants a long life filled with happiness.

Tie Guai Lee, protector of the South, **brings wisdom and healing**. His element is Fire and his symbol is the Bottle Gourd. He is often depicted as an unkempt old man with disheveled hair, taking on the appearance of a beggar. His chosen role is to care for those who are sick, poor or in need.

Enhance for Future Prosperity
in the Northeast

The animal sign of the year, the Ox plays host to the *Future Prosperity Star #9*. This star signifies imminent wealth just about to ripen, and the closer we get to Period 9, which starts Feb 4th 2024, the shorter the waiting time for what is considered "future wealth". The #9 is also a magnifying star, which gains power as we head into Period 9. The Ox sign this year thus gets energized with the presence of this star in its sector. The NE is also the place of the Tiger, who features as always in the year's Paht Chee in the month pillar.

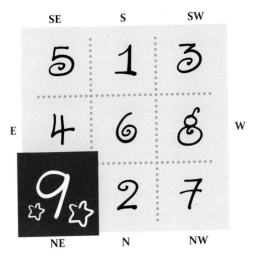

The NE plays host to the "Future Prosperity Star"

The powerful Fire star #9 brings vitality to all who come under its influence, and its presence in the ruling animal sector bodes well for the coming year. This star benefits homes that face NE, and individuals whose bedrooms or office rooms are located NE, as well as those born under the signs of Ox and Tiger.

The #9 in the NE suggests that the central #6 heavenly star gets strengthened. This is a lucky star for most of the year, except for months when monthly flying stars here are unfavourable – i.e. March, May, July, August and December 2021. When unfavourable monthly stars visit, ensure you have the relevant cures in place and keep this sector less active during these times.

ENHANCERS FOR THE NORTHEAST

The NE benefits from the **9 Golden Dragons Plaque** featuring nine celestial Dragons that bestow power and generates the capacity to pursue all one's grandest ambitions conviction and courage.

Having nine Dragons in the NE allows you to stay focused on long-term goals without getting distracted,

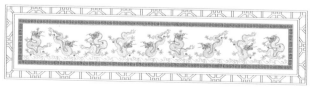

Display the 9 Golden Dragons Plaque in the NE.

or discouraged by short-term difficulties. They protect you against those who wish to see you fail, and shields you from the effects of less ambitious relatives or acquaintances who do not have your vision.

Displaying this plaque in the NE of your home or office ensures you have the support of not one but *nine* Dragons, the number that symbolizes completion and abundance. The number 9 is a magical number as it is a number that always reduces back to itself when multiplied. It also strengthens the #9 star, which is getting stronger as we move rapidly towards a fast-approaching Period of 9.

BUILD YOUR WEALTH: You should also activate the NE with a collection of **Wealth Cabinets**. These wealth cabinets symbolize an accumulation of asset wealth, meaning that the money you make accrues into ever-larger amounts that can last into the many generations. Energizing the NE helps you to make enough money so you do not have to spend everything you earn. It allows you to grow wealthy enough to carve out a secure, comfortable and worry-free future for yourself and your loved ones.

Activate for Love & Romance
in the EAST

The Peach Blossom Star #4 settles into in the East sector this year. This star gets greatly enhanced in 2021 as the East is the place of the Rabbit, the creature associated with the Moon, and with the Goddess of the Moon who governs all fortunes to do with love, romance and relationships. Legend has it that when you catch the attention of the Moon Goddess, she aids you in all matters related to the heart, improving relations between lovers and even matchmaking those who are destined to be together.

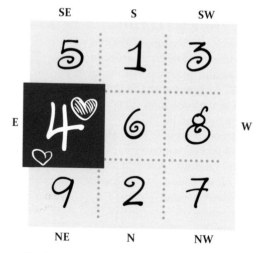

The East plays host to the Peach Blossom Star, which brings romance.

For those who are single, activating this sector with the **Rabbit in the Moon** awakens the powers of **Moon Goddess**, alerting her to all wishes to do with affairs of the heart. Enhancing this sector promotes the success of relationships, attracts marriage opportunities, smooths interactions between spouses, and imbues stale marriages with a newfound passion and vigour.

The EAST becomes the place of the MOON RABBIT in 2021, harnessing the power of the Lunar Mansions to bring great love and romance into the lives of those who activate this luck.

This is the sector to enhance if love is what you are looking for! This year we have designed the **Rabbit in the Moon**, the earthly messenger of this lunar goddess. Placing this activator in the East will help singles meet their soulmates and forever partners, while helping those who are already married to keep their spouses. Remember that this year's Paht Chee generates the unfavourable *External Flower of Romance Star*, which can cause problems within already existing relationships, resulting in unwanted love triangles and other outside disturbances to a love relationship. Invoking the blessings of the **Rabbit in the Moon** ensures that only the positive aspects of love materialize. It will also protect against unpleasantness associated with matters of the heart. They say there is nothing sweeter than love, but they also say that nothing breaks like a heart – remember the song by Mark Ronson and Miley Cyrus? Heartache and heartbreak can be far more painful than physical pain; the #4 in the East brings the Moon Rabbit to life and provides a solution for those looking for happiness in love.

ATTRACTING MARRIAGE OPPORTUNITIES

For those looking for a soul mate, someone you can settle down with and make a future with, or if you are already dating but your partner seems a long way off from proposing marriage, you can speed things along with the help of your **Peach Blossom Animal**. Our new Peach Blossom animals the **Rat**, **Rabbit**, **Horse** and **Rooster** come with trees of fortune enhanced with potent symbols of love and marriage. The **Peach Blossom Rat** brings love and marriage opportunities to the **Boar**, **Rabbit** and **Sheep**. If you are looking for love that leads to marriage or you would like your current partner to propose, display a **Peach Blossom Rat** in the NORTH, or in the EAST in 2021.

Peach Blossom Rat

For students,
activate the Scholastic Star in the EAST

For young people and anyone pursuing their studies, engaged in research or in search of new knowledge, they can activate the scholastic star of the year which flies to the East in 2021. The #4 is also the star number that brings study and exam luck; when properly activated, it has the power to help you achieve success in anything related to scholastic accolades. Enhancing this star improves clarity of mind, allowing you to absorb new knowledge and to process it with much greater efficiency. Anything requiring cognitive

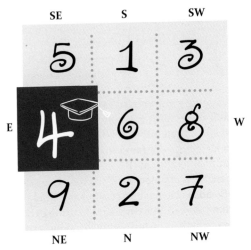

The #4 star in the East is also the Star of Scholarship

reasoning and abilities gets enhanced when you harness the energies of this star number.

The #4 Scholastic Star also boosts creativity and original thinking, allowing you to better come up with unique and innovative new ideas. This star gets strengthened this year, as it is a Wood star flying into a Wood sector.

ENHANCE THE SCHOLASTIC STAR: The best way to activate the #4 for scholastic luck is to carry **Manjushri's Gau**. Manjushri is the Buddha of Wisdom, and when you call on his help, he slices through your ignorance so only wisdom remains. His flaming sword removes all that is obscured in your mind, allowing you to think with a clear head so you can map out effective solutions to everything you are pursuing.

For students taking exams, having Manjushri's support enables them to recall everything they have revised and studied, and to write excellent answers in their exam. Manjushri boosts everything to do with wisdom and intelligence, and helps one to make wise choices. He ensures one constantly sees the big picture, while also filling in the details. For school-going children, they can clip **Manjushri's Amulet** onto their schoolbag. The specially-designed **Scholastic Amulet with Manjushri's mantra** sums up all of his wisdom and blessings, providing an endless stream of support, reinforcement and inspiration.

FOR EXAM LUCK:

For students taking important exams and hoping to do well, there is no better enhancer than the **Dragon Carp**. The carp that jumps over the Dragon Gate and successfully transforms into a Dragon is the best symbol of success for anyone aspiring to scholastic success. It promotes the luck of the scholarship and helps students not just pass exams but excel in them. The Dragon Carp also generates a strong sense of self-motivation, ensuring one does not fall into bad company or get side-tracked into unproductive tasks. This is the best enhancer for children or teenagers looking to perform well in important exams, to win awards, to gain scholarships and grants and to gain admission into colleges of their choice.

The academic path of today is filled with potholes and pitfalls, far more than in the old days, as everything has become so much more competitive. More and more young people are fighting for fewer places at the top universities and colleges; at school, children are faced with competition from classmates with Tiger parents in the sidelines egging them on. For a young mind, it can all become too much, and with all the expectations heaped on young shoulders these days, sometimes all it takes is one bad test or one bad result to cause a child to throw in the towel and just give up.

As parents, we need to imbue in our children not just the impetus to keep striving for the top, but help them understand there will be bumps and disappointments along the way. It is not necessary to perform every single day of the year, to come out top in every single test; what is important is to peak when it counts. The **Dragon Carp** stabilizes one's mind, helping a child along the academic path and to navigate all that comes his or her way with a strong and mature mind, resulting in success when it truly matters.

Transform Five Yellow Misfortune Star
in the Southeast

The bogus star, the Five Yellow, makes its way into the Southeast this year. The good news is that because the Southeast is a Wood Sector, it mitigates the extent of damage of this dangerous Earth star, as Wood destroys Earth in the cycle of elements. When the Five Yellow flies into a Wood sector, misfortune can be turned into opportunity. This is why we have designed this year's **Five Element Pagoda with a Tree of Life**. This alters the effects of the *wu wang*, suppressing the darker side of this star while

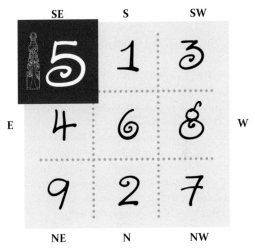

	SE	S	SW
	5	1	3
E	4	6	8	W
	9	2	7
	NE	N	NW

The 5 Yellow afflicts the SE in 2021 but with the correct cure, this Five Yellow has the potential to bring great good luck!

harnessing its benevolent powers. This star affects those living in homes that face SE, those with bedrooms or work rooms in the SE, and those born in years of the Dragon and Snake.

If your house has more than one level, make sure you have a **Five Element Pagoda with Tree of Life** on every floor. Keep the SE of the home free from too much activity and noise, and avoid renovations in this part of the home in 2021. Whatever you do, DO NOT renovate the SE of the home this year.

Victory Star brings winning luck
to the South

The White Star #1 associated with victory and winning luck makes its way to the South. This star allows you to triumph in any situation and to attain success over any competition you may face. In 2021, this star benefits those whose bedrooms are located South, and all those living in homes that face South. Anyone who spends a lot of time in this part of their home can also tap into the good luck this star brings by keeping it well energized with the correct activators. The livelier you keep this part of the home, the better!

The South sector enjoys the Victory Star in 2021.

The Victory Star this year is made more potent as it is supported by not one but **TWO Big Auspicious Stars** from the 24 Mountains, as well as the **Golden Deity Star**, echoing the benefits of the ruling star of the year, the #6 Heaven Star. All this serves to increase the power and effectiveness of this star, so it is really worthwhile to actively enhance this star this year. Because the South is the sector governing the reputation of the household, the #1 here also improves one's standing and repute in various circles – work, social, etc.

ACTIVATE THE VICTORY STAR:
The best enhancer for the Victory Star is the **Victorious Windhorse Carrying a Jewel**. The Windhorse is the very essence of success luck, known as the magical steed of the folk hero King Gesar, who when riding his Windhorse could never be defeated. His horse with flaming red coat has become synonymous with success and victory, and his image is what is needed whenever one needs to boost one's chances against others in any kind of competitive situation. In 2021, we recommend for everyone to place the Victorious Windhorse in the South. This sector is also the home sector of the Horse, an auspicious creature that emanates pure Fire energy. Displaying images and figurines of horses in the South is thus very appropriate and auspicious indeed.

Activate the #1 Star in the South with the Victorious Windhorse

BOOST POWER AND AUTHORITY:
For those in positions of leadership and management, the best way to enhance your effectiveness as a leader is with the help of the **Ru Yi**. The Ru Yi is the royal scepter of power, which bestows "the right to rule". In ancient China, anyone in any kind of power would never be seen without a Ru Yi at his side. You can place your Ru Yi in front of you on your work desk, or carry in your bag.

The **Crimson Red Ru Yi with Bats** brings the luck of **success and abundance**. Any boss, head or leader can use the help of this Ru Yi to ensure things between all in their group stay harmonious, joyful and productive at all times. It attracts the luck of abundance and success, so whatever is pursued turns out fruitful and effective. It helps you to ensure all your final goals are reached in the most harmonious way.

Anyone in any kind of leadership position needs a Ru Yi.

The **Deep Blue Ru Yi with 8 Auspicious Symbols** brings the luck of **wealth**. This Ru Yi includes the Victory Banner for winning luck, the Double Fish for abundance, the Parasol for protection, the Conch for good news, the Wheel for sustainability, the Mystic Knot for longevity, the Vase for completion and the Lotus for good intentions.

These symbols of good fortune are the magical implements of the Eight Immortals, and act as vessels of their power. Carrying images of their magical symbols on a Ru Yi imbues you with a complete collection of the different kinds of luck you need to reach your full potential as a leader.

The **Yellow Ru Yi with Celestial Dragon** brings the luck of **power and position**. Those operating in political environments or in politics need this Ru Yi! It bestows charisma and magnetism, and endows strength to make your position one that is stable and secure. It ensures you do not get plotted against and overthrown. It protects against betrayal and treachery and gives you power over those on the outside as well as on the inside.

The SOUTH is the place to activate if success, victory, fame and reputation is what you seek.

Suppress the Quarrelsome Star
in the Southwest

The Quarrelsome Star #3 flies to the Southwest, bringing hostile energy and complications associated with arguments, misunderstandings and court cases. The #3 star can also cause serious aggravations that lead to violence and tragedy. This affliction affects anyone with a bedroom in the SW, those whose main doors face SW, and those born in years of the Sheep and Monkey. It also affects the Matriarch of the

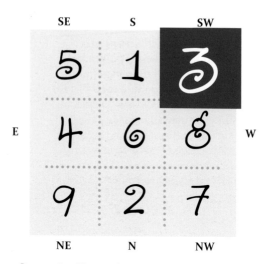

	SE	S	SW	
	5	1	3	
E	4	6	8	W
	9	2	7	
	NE	N	NW	

Beware the #3 quarrelsome star in the SW this year.

household. The #3 star is especially strong this year, as the intrinsic Wood energy of the star dominates the Earth energy of the SW. The effects of this star are made worse as the SW also plays host to the **Yin House** from the 24 Mountains. All this suggests that this affliction MUST be taken seriously.

Anything that suggests Fire is an effective cure, so keeping the lights turned on brightly in this sector will help combat the negative energies of this star. **The colour red** is also suitable, so red curtains, rugs and cushion covers here will help very much indeed.

CURES FOR THE QUARRELSOME STAR:
For 2021, the best remedy for the Quarrelsome Star in the SW is the **Nine Phoenix Plaque** in red and gold. These celestial birds in red and gold - which represent the elements of Fire and Metal - work to subdue this troublesome Wood Star. The Fire energy engulfs the Wood of the #3, while the Metal energy of the gold effectively subdues it.

The Nine Phoenix Plaque is an excellent cure against the #3 Quarrelsome Star.

We also recommend placing **red carpets** in this sector, or in the SW portion of any room you spend a lot of time in. Another effective cure for the #3 are the **Red Peace and Harmony Apples**. In Chinese, the word for peaceful is *Ping*, which sounds like the word for apple – *Ping Kor*. This year's Peace Apples comes embossed with the English word "Peace" and the Chinese rhyming couplet carrying the meaning "If your intentions are good and your heart is pure, the world will be peaceful."

Place this pair of apples in the SW to ensure all members of the household stay supportive of one another, and to prevent clashes and conflict from arising. Also an excellent cure for use within the office to maintain a productive and supportive environment between colleagues and workmates.

Enhance Prosperity Star 8
in the West

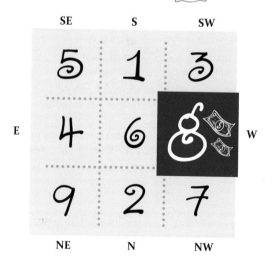

The Wealth Star #8 flies to the West this year.

The very lucky Wealth Star #8 makes its way to the West, the sector of the Rooster. This star is also known as the *Current Prosperity Star*, as we are currently in the Period of 8. The West is the sector that represents children and descendants, suggesting that the wealth this sector brings will last into the long term, reaching future generations and for many generations to come. It points to a successful accumulation of assets over time if properly energized.

In 2021, the West can be considered one of the luckiest areas of the home, because it enjoys this auspicious #8 star. The strong energy of the current period emanating from this sector benefits all homes whose main entrances face West, and all bedrooms and offices located in the West benefit from this luck. The West is also the place of the youngest daughter, so the wealth this sector brings benefits the young girls of the house.

WEALTH luck takes root in the WEST sector this year, so this is the area of the home you should enhance for greater prosperity luck.

Remember that to activate the luck of this auspicious star #8, the West should be thoroughly imbued with yang energy - this means lots of activity, lots of noise and plenty of bright lights. When there is movement, sound, chatter and merry-making, the number 8 comes to life, bringing good fortune and big prosperity. In the constellations, 8 is a "man-made star" with two assistants – on the right and on the left - so that at its strongest moments, it brings wealth and great nobility.

When the 8 can turn dangerous...

Beware however. The number becomes negative when afflicted by structures in the environment that threaten its location. If the West sector of your home has too much Metal energy, or if there are harmful physical structures that cause poison arrows to direct threatening energy your way, that is when the number 8 can bring harm to young children especially young daughters of the household, causing illness to arise. If there are such structures external to your home,

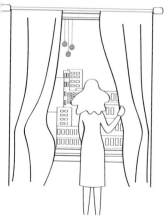

but towards the West, it is important to block the view with curtains, or dissipate the killing energy with **facetted crystal balls**. These will disperse the worst of the killing breath before it has the chance to enter your home.

If the view from your window to the WEST is of a threatening looking building with sharp edges or poison arrows, keep the curtains in this area closed to block the offending view from spoiling your feng shui. Hang facetted crystal balls here.

ACTIVATE FOR WEALTH IN THE WEST

The best way to manifest wealth luck in 2021 is the make sure the West part of your home is well-energized with wealth symbols. Because this is the year of the Ox, this creature is especially lucky as it symbolizes harnessing the good fortune of the year. Because the West represents children and descendants, this prosperity luck benefits the whole family not just in the present but into the long term.

The image of the Ox has great power to attract abundant good fortune in 2021. Displaying images of the Ox in all sizes and permutations is so lucky this year! For the collectors among you, a good time to start "collecting" Ox images.

A fabulous wealth enhancer for this year is the **Asset Wealth Bull**. This Bull holds the symbolic and subliminal message "May the market bull for you"! With resplendent red saddle and surrounded by coins, ingots and symbols of prosperity, this bull energizes for wealth of the kind that can accumulate into expanded net worth, the kind that provides meaningful disposable income, providing a worry-free future.

Display the Asset Wealth Bull for wealth that grows and expands your net worth!

To tap the hidden wealth of the year, display the **Ox Finding Hidden Wealth**. This Ox is depicting calmly and unobtrusively grazing in a field full of coins, sniffing out hidden wealth and opportunities. In a year with little obvious wealth but a lot of hidden wealth, this Ox generates the luck that allows you to tap the full potential of the year.

Invite in the "Ox Finding Hidden Wealth" to tap the full potential of the year.

Another great activator for this year's wealth star is the **Tree Bringing 3 Kinds of Wealth**.

Trees always depict growth energy, and when they look like money trees, they really do bring the luck of wealth into the home! Our tree this year has been designed to represent the manifestation of 3 different kinds of wealth - Asset Wealth, Income Wealth and Growth Wealth. Having all three kinds of wealth brings you not just enough to lead a comfortable life now, it gives you security and peace of mind and allows you to plan for the future. This year's wealth tree also features 12 lucky charms to signify abundance in all forms entering your life - the Double Fish, the Apple, the Treasure Chest, the Golden Ingot, the Wealth Vase, the Abacus, the I-Ching Coin, Gold bars, the 4-leafed clover the Maneki Neko Lucky Cat and the Pot of Gold.

This year's wealth tree represents not just prosperity luck but also the luck of asset accumulation. This symbolises your wealth growing and your networth expanding.

Beware Betrayal & Loss Star
in the Northwest

A dangerous aspect of this year's chart is the #7 Robbery Star in the NW. This brings loss and betrayal energies to the Patriarch, which not only means the patriarch of the family, but leaders, bosses, managers and anyone responsible for the welfare or livelihood of others. The presence of the #7 in the NW suggests that the Patriarch could get cheated, conned or betrayed. It brings the energy that suggests you should keep your friends close but your enemies closer.

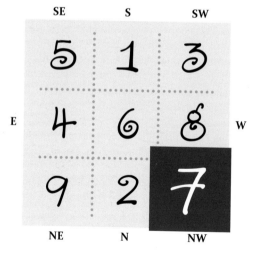

The NW, the sector of the Patriarch and Leader, gets afflicted by the #7 Loss and Betrayal Star in 2021.

In 2021, keep your friends close but your enemies closer!

Stay alert like a hawk, as treachery can strike at any moment. The energies of the year could corrupt even the most trustworthy of friends and the most loyal of employees. The #7 Robbery Star, like its namesake, describes a situation when you are cheated out of money; but it can also manifest as an actual robbery. We recommend all who stay out late, or who venture anywhere even remotely unsafe, to carry the **Nightspot Protection Amulet**. Because this star affects the NW, it harms the Father the most, but there can be knock-on adverse effects on the rest of the family, or the rest of a leader's charges.

CURE FOR #7 STAR: This year the best cure for the #7 star in the home is the **Anti-Burglary Plaque with Door Guardians**. These Door Gods with spear in the ready are depicted with the Anti-Burglary Amulets, with the Chinese proverb, "May your family be blessed with peace, safety and abundant joy, may your home be filled with everlasting happiness."

Display in the NW to ensure your home stays protected against unexpected and unwanted intruders, who may cause not just loss of property and possessions, but loss of peace of mind. These door guardians will help keep your family protected through the year.

BEWARE BETRAYAL:

This year, risk of betrayal is rife as the #7 star occupies the NW, the location of the leader. Betrayal means duplicity from those you trust, those you least suspect and therefore those you are most vulnerable to. While it feels nasty to get cheated by conmen and people you do not know, when betrayals come from those closest to you, the harm is emotional as well as physical. The loss is no longer merely monetary, it hits a nerve deep within that can be difficult to take and recover from. This year, because opportunity for this to happen gets increased, we suggest to remove temptation where you can, watch your back, and carry symbols to protect against this kind of bad luck. Carry the **Kuan Kung Anti-Betrayal Amulet**. This specially-designed talisman features the amulet that protects against being stabbed in the back, with the mantra that ensures the protection is effective.

Kuan Kung
Anti-Betrayal Amulet

PROTECT AGAINST BEING CHEATED:
For those engaging in high-risk deals, carry the **Anti-Cheating Amulet** to ensure you do not get conned by unscrupulous people. An excellent amulet for business people and for anyone dealing with new acquaintances who may be untrustworthy.

PROTECTION AGAINST THE DARK ARTS:
Another form of harm can come from those who practice black magic. Especially in the East, such arts are more common than you think. Even if you do not subscribe or "believe" in this kind of power, it exists. Someone who projects negative thoughts against you, whether out of spite, jealousy or some other reason, does not even have to be skilled in these methods to send negative hexes and projectiles your way!

For example, if someone curses you on the street because they are angry at the way you drive, this can result in the same kind of misfortune effect as someone actively plotting or using black magic against you. The latter is of course more serious, but whenever one is weak in terms of spirit essence and element luck, they can succumb badly when someone forms negative thoughts and sends those thoughts their way.

The best protection against this kind of harm is the **28 Hums Protection Wheel**, which features the powerful **Heart Sutra** on the back. These sacred syllables together with this powerful sutra ensures that whatever projectiles are sent your way cannot reach you. A vital cure for anyone with enemies, who are engaged in high stakes deals, or anyone who may have offended someone intentionally or unintentionally.

28 Hums
Protection Wheel

Suppress Illness Star
in the North

The #2 Illness Star flies to the North, and because North is of the Water element, it cannot do anything on its own to weaken the energies of the #2, an Earth star. The Illness Star is further strengthened as it is supported by the **Yin House Star** in North 2, the sector of the Rat. This boosts the potency of this star, making the North sector dangerous for those who are elderly, frail or prone to illness.

It is important for anyone whose bedroom is facing North, or whose home faces North to suppress the Illness Star with strong cures.

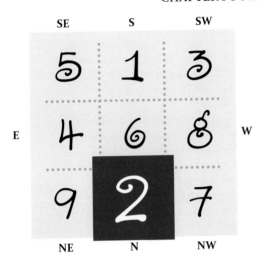

SE 5	**S** 1	**SW** 3
E 4	6	8 **W**
NE 9	**N** 2	**NW** 7

The North gets afflicted by the Illness Star this year.

CURE FOR THE ILLNESS STAR:
In 2021, a good cure for the Illness Star is the **Healing Deer Carrying Vase of Longevity with Linzhi**. The deer is renowned by the Chinese for their powerful curative properties and is often seen as the companion of the God of Longevity, Sau Seng Kong. With the world caught up in fears of epidemics and pandemics where there seems no escape with a proper cure a long time coming, the

Healing Deer

deer is an excellent shield against this kind of illness. Display in the North of the home this year. The Healing Deer is an excellent symbol of good health in the year 2021.

Another potent cure against the Illness Star #2 is the **Medicine Buddha & 7 Sugatas Gau**. Medicine Buddha always comes to the aid of those who are suffering when one calls for his help. His area of expertise is in the removal of poisons, disease and illness, and the **Medicine Buddha & 7 Sugatas Gau** features all 8 of his emanations, and his powerful mantras in whole. You can place in the North of the home to stay under his protection constantly. Excellent for anyone who is ill or feeling unwell.

You can also chant his mantra daily:
TADYATHA OM BHEKHANDZYE BHEKHANDZYE MAHA BHEKHANDZYE (BHEKHANDZYE) RADZA SAMUGATE SOHA

For those suffering from a chronic ailment, we suggest that you get yourself a dedicated **Medicine Buddha Mala** to chant with. The more you chant his mantra over the mala, the more powerful the mala will become. Keep the mala with you always, and whenever you have spare time, bring it out and chant. You can also wear the mala as an accessory around your wrist or neck.

HEART MANTRA
OF ARYA VAIROCHANA
WOFS™

AGAINST COVID-19: To protect against the coronavirus specifically, the best cure is to invite in an image of the **Buddha Vairocana**, who brings blessings of good health but also provides strong protection against contagious diseases. Display his image as a figurine, and also carry his image in the form of a **Gold Talisman Card** which we have made available to help tide us through these challenging times.

AFFLICTIONS OF 2021
TAI SUI *in the NORTHEAST*

The TAI SUI or God of the Year always occupies the sector of the ruling animal sign of the year. This year, he occupies the palace of the Ox, Northeast 1. The Tai Sui is the celestial force that governs all that happens on Earth, and when one has his support and blessings, very little can go wrong, but when one offends him, his wrath knows no bounds.

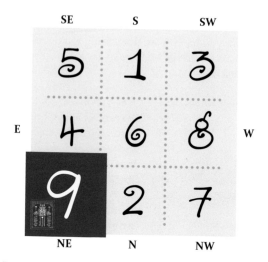

The Tai Sui resides in the NE this year, and it is important to keep him on your side. Place the Tai Sui Plaque 2021 here.

It is a matter of course and tradition for most Chinese who believe, to offer prayers to Tai Sui at the start of the year, humbly asking for his help and support for the coming year. In feng shui, the creature that is known to appease him is the celestial chimera the **Dragon Pi Xie**, so we always recommend to place this in the location of the Tai Sui.

The Dragon Pi Xie is said to appease the Tai Sui. Place in the NE in 2021.

PROTECTION: What is even more important is to place the **Tai Sui Plaque** with his image and invocation as a sign of respect. In 2021, place this in the NE1 sector. Animal signs especially affected by the Tai Sui this year

are the Earth signs of Sheep, Dragon and Dog, while the Ox whose location he occupies should also be mindful of his presence there. For these 4 signs, we also recommend carrying the **Tai Sui Amulet** at all times throughout the year.

THREE KILLINGS in the EAST

This affliction is said to bring three types of misfortune – loss of wealth, loss of reputation and loss of a loved one. All three are devastating, and when not one but three forms of bad luck hit you at once, the loss can be difficult and extremely distressing This is another affliction that is important to take note of and to cure.

Firstly, NEVER have your back to the Three Killings affliction, so in 2021, DO NOT SIT FACING WEST,

EVEN if WEST is your best direction! Do not sit with your back to the East, as the Three Killings is the kind of affliction that stabs you in the back, when you are least suspecting. It carries the characteristic of hitting you when you are most comfortable and least aware. When things are at their calmest, beware, because the storm is about to pound and crash down.

NEVER HAVE YOUR BACK TO THE EAST this year! Make sure you do not get stabbed by the dangerous 3 killings affliction!

CURE FOR THE THREE KILLINGS: Place the **3 Celestial Shields** to combat the Three Killings.

These shields act as effective armour sheltering you from the effects of this difficult affliction. All homes should display these shields in the EAST of the home in 2021. Anyone with something to lose, who operate where stakes are high, or who are going through years of low element luck are also recommended to carry the **3 Celestial Shields Amulet** when on the go. Use as a keychain or bag decoration.

Compatibilities with other Signs in 2021

Chapter 5

Boar benefits from being surrounded by the right people

The Boar in 2021 has the difficult Loss Star to contend with, so your focus is unlikely to be primarily on love. You have other things on your mind, and your variable mood may scare potential suitors away. Yet you benefit from having allies, supporters and yes, even a healthy love life! The best advice for the Boar this year is to fall back on your intrinsic easy-going nature. Don't worry too much when things seem down. When you look at the cup half full rather than half empty, things magically improve in all of life and definitely in all your relationships.

Many different influences come into play each year to determine how one animal sign gets along with another. Chinese astrology has so many permutations that it is difficult to take note of everything, but examining some of the main variables can give useful insights to the general mood and compatibility between any two signs in any year. The annual energies of the year have a larger bearing on the effect on your relationships than you may be aware of, and understanding these effects allows you to be more effective in all your interactions.

When you find the keys to unlock what makes your connections tick, not only will this help with your happiness levels, it also improves your productivity and success potential.

Every animal sign under the Chinese Zodiac system has certain signs they are naturally drawn towards; certain signs make better spouses, others make more exciting lovers, others still work better when you remain platonic friends. Certain pairings thrive in a business relationship, as boss and employee, mentor and mentee; others work well as parent and child, siblings, sporting teammates or drinking buddies; while others still, have the potential to change your life in a big way.

There are also certain signs you need to stay alert to and be wary of. One's Zodiac Adversary is the animal sign born six years apart from you, the sign directly opposite you in the Zodiac wheel – but in certain years, your "natural enemy" can become a useful ally, while in others, you would be best advised to stay well clear of each other. Having knowledge of how the year's energies influence your relationships will give you the edge when it comes to how you relate to others in any given year.

In this section, we analyse the relationship between the Boar and the other signs of the Zodiac, looking in particular at the quality and nature of the relationships as determined by the influences of 2021.

1. Alliance of Allies

There are four affinity groupings that form natural allies in the horoscope. The three signs in each group

ALLY GROUPINGS	ANIMALS	CHARACTERISTICS
Competitors	Rat, Dragon, Monkey	Competent, Tough, Resolute
Intellectuals	Ox, Snake, Rooster	Generous, Focused, Resilient
Enthusiasts	Dog, Tiger, Horse	Aggressive, Rebellious, Coy
Diplomats	Boar, Sheep, Rabbit	Creative, Kind, Emotional

have similar thought processes, aspirations and goals.
Their attitudes are alike, and their support of each
other is immediate and instinctive. If there is an alliance
within a family unit amongst siblings, or between
spouses and their child, the family is incredibly
supportive, giving strength to each other. In good years,
auspicious luck gets multiplied.

Astrological allies always get along. Any falling out
is temporary. They trust each other and close ranks
against external threats. Good astrological feng shui
comes from carrying the image of your allies, especially
when they are going through good years.

When all three signs in a particular year has good
fortune, the alliance is strengthened. But in years when
one sign stands out with superior luck, the others in
its grouping can "lean" on that sign to lift itself up.
The Boar belongs to the grouping of Diplomats in the
Zodiac, comprising the Rabbit, Sheep and Boar.

This year, the strongest link in the
Boar's alliance of allies is the Rabbit,
who has the most promising element luck
in the group. For the Boar, friends born
in years of the Rabbit brings you good
fortune luck in 2021.

In 2021, the Boar can lean on the Rabbit to gain strength. It favours the Boar to fraternize with friends born in the year of the Rabbit, who brings new opportunities to its ally the Boar. The excellent element luck of your friend the Rabbit gives you a boost of confidence and a line to significant contacts and opportunities.

If you do not have close friends or alliances born in a Rabbit year, you can simulate this luck by displaying images or figurines of the Rabbit in your home. Hang beautiful and inspiring art of the Rabbit in your home, or display auspicious Rabbit depictions. The Rabbit when depicted with the moon attracts romance luck to singles and long-lasting happiness to those already married.

People born under the Rabbit sign
are very good for the Boar in 2021.

2. Zodiac Soulmates

Another natural ally for you is your Zodiac soulmate. In Chinese astrology, there are six pairs of signs that create six Zodiac Houses of yin and yang soulmates. Each pair creates powerful bonding on a cosmic level. Marriages or business unions between people belonging to the same Zodiac House are extremely auspicious. In a marriage, there is great love and devotion, and in a commercial partnership, it promises much wealth and success. Such a pairing is also good between professional colleagues or between siblings.

The strength of each pair is different, each having a defining strength with some making better commercial than marriage partners. How successful you are as a pair depends on how you bond. The table on the following page summarizes the key strength of each Zodiac house.

For the Boar, your Zodiac Soulmate is the Dog. Together, you form the *House of Domesticity*. This is a wonderful alliance that generates beautiful family harmony because these are two animal signs for whom domestic bliss is more important than anything else. Family is extremely important to you both, so the bond you share is strong and powerfully loyal. A marriage between the two of you is certain to be harmonious and happy.

HOUSES OF PAIRED SOULMATES

ANIMALS	YIN/YANG	ZODIAC HOUSE	TARGET UNLEASHED
Rat & Ox	YANG /YIN	*House of Creativity & Cleverness*	The Rat initiates The Ox completes
Tiger & Rabbit	YANG /YIN	*House of Growth & Development*	The Tiger uses strength The Rabbit uses negotiation
Dragon & Snake	YANG /YIN	*House of Magic & Spirituality*	The Dragon takes action The Snake creates magic
Horse & Sheep	YANG /YIN	*House of Passion & Sexuality*	The Horse embodies strength & courage The Sheep embodies seduction & allure
Monkey & Rooster	YANG /YIN	*House of Career & Commerce*	The Monkey creates good strategy The Rooster takes timely action
Dog & Boar	YANG /YIN	*House of Domesticity*	The Dog creates alliances The Boar benefits

In 2021 however, both Boar and Dog are not feeling particularly upbeat, but despite difficulties this year, you should make every effort to work through any issues, as in the long run, this pairing is extremely beneficial for you both. Should you be in a commercial arrangement with one another, it benefits Dog to trust the Boar to get the job done. This is not a year for the Dog to be too active in business.

3. Secret Friends

Another extremely powerful affinity arises when two secret friends come together. There are six pairs of secret friends in the Zodiac. Love, respect and goodwill flow freely between you. Once forged, your bond is extremely hard to break. Even when you yourselves want to break it, it will be hard for either party to walk away. This pair of signs will stick together through thick and thin. For the Boar, your secret friend is the

PAIRINGS OF SECRET FRIENDS			
🐀	Rat	Ox	🐂
🐖	Boar	Tiger	🐅
🐕	Dog	Rabbit	🐇
🐉	Dragon	Rooster	🐓
🐍	Snake	Monkey	🐒
🐎	Horse	Sheep	🐐

Tiger. The Boar's flair for networking and the Tiger's powerful determination make you a masterful couple, and coupled with that, plenty of love and lust for life and each other. 2021 brings Tiger the luck of *Small Auspicious*, while Boar has both *Small and Big Auspicious*. When you pair up, your combination generates good fortune in spades. This is a relationship that is equally beneficially for both!

4. Peach Blossom Links

Each alliance of allies has a special relationship with one of the four primary signs of Horse, Rat, Rooster and Rabbit in that these are the symbolic representations of love and romance for one alliance group of animal signs. These are referred to as *Peach Blossom Animals*, and the presence of their images in the homes of the matching alliance of allies brings peach blossom luck, which is associated with love and romance.

> The Boar belongs to the alliance of Rabbit, Sheep and Boar, which has the Rat as their Peach Blossom link.

The Boar benefits from displaying images of the Peach Blossom Rat in the home, which brings love and marriage opportunities into your life. Place the **Peach Blossom Rat** in the North of your home for romance luck this year.

5. Seasonal Trinities

Another grouping of signs creates the seasonal trinity combinations that bring the luck of *seasonal abundance*. To many experts, this is regarded as one of the more powerful combinations. When it exists within a family made up of either parent or both parents with one or more children, it indicates that as a family unit, their collective luck can transform all that is negative into positive outcomes. When annual indications of the year are not favourable, the existence of a seasonal combination of signs in any living abode can transform bad luck into better luck, especially during the season indicated by the combination.

It is necessary for all three signs to live together or be in the same office working in close proximity for this powerful pattern to work.

ANIMAL SIGNS	SEASON	ELEMEMT	DIRECTION
Dragon, Rabbit, Tiger	*Spring*	Wood	East
Snake, Horse, Sheep	*Summer*	Fire	South
Monkey, Rooster, Dog	*Autumn*	Metal	West
Ox, Rat, Boar	*Winter*	Water	North

Seasonal Trinities

6. Astrological Enemies

Your astrological enemy is the sign that directly confronts yours in the astrology wheel. For the Boar, your astrological enemy is the Snake. Note that your enemy does not necessarily harm you; it only means someone of this sign can never be of any real help to you. There is a six year gap between natural enemies. A marriage between astrological enemies is not usually recommended. Thus marriage between a Boar and Snake is unlikely to bring happiness unless other indications suggest otherwise. The Boar is advised to refrain from getting involved with anyone born in the year of the Snake, although on a year-by-year basis, this can sometimes be overcome by the annual energies.

As a business partnership, an adversary pairing is likely to lead to problems, and in the event of a split, the separation is often acrimonious. Even if passion flows

PAIRINGS OF ASTROLOGICAL ENEMIES		
Rat	⟷	Horse
Boar	⟷	Snake
Dog	⟷	Dragon
Rabbit	⟷	Rooster
Tiger	⟷	Monkey
Ox	⟷	Sheep

between you at the early stages of your relationship, you are not likely to be happy in the long run.

Boar and Snake are better off not marrying or living together as partners. Even when there is love flowing back and forth during the initial stages, you are unlikely to be close over the long term. Note however that astrological opposites can co-exist quite harmoniously as friends or siblings.

> **CURE:** If a Boar is already married to a Snake, the solution to improve your prospects for lasting happiness is to introduce the secret friend of each other into your living space. This can be done through the symbolic use of figurines or art. As a pair, you should thus display the secret friend of the Snake, the **Monkey**, and the secret friend of the Boar, the **Tiger**, in the home, together with your own signs of **Boar** and **Snake**.

Secret Friends

Secret Friends

BOAR with RAT

Water friends so good for one another

These seasonal friends are both Winter creatures who share much in common when it comes to their interests and sense of humour. They think the same way, laugh at the same things, and have goals and aspirations that line up perfectly. Boar and Rat will always be friends no matter what the circumstance. Because they are also part of the seasonal trinity of Winter, when involved with one another in a commercial or business sense, their greatest success comes during the season of Winter.

In 2021, Boar and Rat share more than just seasonal compatibility with one another. Their energies combine to form the auspicious sum-of-ten! This means that whatever joint projects they undertake will meet with success. Wealth in particular becomes an easy aspiration to achieve together.

In love, Boar and Rat are so very comfortable with one another that building a happy home and family life comes as second nature. Both are sociable creatures, but neither are the madly social type chasing status or glamour on the society scene. For both, while they enjoy the company of friends, prefer the more down-to-earth variety of parties and get-togethers, like game nights at each other's homes, or family get-togethers with the extended clan.

Neither Boar nor Rat are madly ambitious when chasing career success, so neither will happily forgo family time to put into a demanding job. They are both happiest as entrepreneurs running their own show or working for a company that allows them time to pursue a life outside of work. Because both think this way, a marriage between Boar and Rat will tend to be happy, domestic and full of children and laughter.

As pals, Boar and Rat are the Bill and Ted of the real world. They drink, dine, laugh and travel together. In 2021, neither Boar nor Rat have very strong element luck, but they weather their lack of energy together, picking activities they are comfortable with which do not exert so much of their energy.

While they are the easy-going pair of the zodiac, they are fiercely loyal and will go to great lengths to defend each other at the slightest whiff of any external threat. If anyone dares defame or badmouth either Boar or Rat, they will have to watch out for the wrath of the other who becomes a self-appointed protector. A wonderful and loving relationship that is extremely auspicious in 2021, but also in any other year.

BOAR with OX
Not the best of times for these two

These two have the potential to make the sweetest of couples, but 2021 does not make this easy for them. The Boar's conflict star makes it difficult to get along with, so the Ox, while usually fond of its easy-going friend, will find Boar's laidback ways bothersome and exasperating.

Under normal circumstances, Ox appreciates Boar's friendly demeanour, but this year, it views Boar as being overly open with others, and a tad too sociable. Boar meanwhile, usually appreciative of a steady Ox partner, finds the Ox stifling and repressive.

The energies of 2021 do nothing to help this otherwise promising pair. Ox has far better luck than Boar, and could view a Boar partner as extra luggage it does not need.

In love, Boar and Ox are in danger of external troublemakers. If you do end up fighting, best to take time to calm down rather than running straight into the arms of another, quite possibly an instigator stoking problems between you. The Flower of Romance star does not favour the Boar and Ox pair, and could cause romantic love triangles that threaten to ruin things for

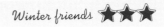

good. Boar and Ox can fight and argue, rant and rave, but neither will accept infidelity. If one or the other succumbs to being unfaithful, it could spell the end of the road even for the longest-standing marriage or partnership.

As colleagues at work, Boar and Ox meet with competitive pressures and could find themselves pitted against each other on different sides. It becomes easy to go from allies to rivals in a heartbeat when prodded and fanned by somebody with something to gain.

Boar and Ox will have to work hard this year to rebuild their usual trust in one another. While these two signs are usually so harmonious together, unfortunately, in 2021, communication begins to break down.

When things get difficult, the less said the better. There is a tendency to say the wrong thing at the wrong time, and then a small problem gets blown out of proportion, becoming uncharacteristically big. If either are having money problems, the fights can get quite nasty. Big-heartedness and plenty of generosity of spirit is needed for this pairing to work this year, and this needs to begin with the Ox.

BOAR with TIGER

Always making the best of things together

This is one of the better pairings of the Zodiac, as Boar and Tiger are not only secret friends, but also very easy-going people who know how to have a good time. Boar and Tiger make a successful match anytime, anyplace!

Boar and Tiger are extroverts who feel secure with one another. Between them are none of the suspicions that afflict other pairings, and this enables them to develop genuine trust that help them make it through troubled times.

Both easily forgive and excuse each other's eccentricities, seeing instead the lighter side of one another's behaviour. These two signs love each other so much that they weather any storms together not just with strength but with joy. Whatever difficulties one faces becomes a joint challenge for both, and they stand by each other's side no matter what it is they are facing. What is so charming is that this couple really find each other attractive and captivating. Theirs is a love match that has great potential to last. It is easy for Boar and Tiger to make a lifetime commitment to one another, as between them is a rare passion that generates a great deal of happiness.

In 2021, Tiger has better flying star luck, but both have auspicious stars brought by the 24 Mountains. When they have each other, they are able to draw out all that is auspicious from the year, because they provide each other with emotional support, and regularly boost each other's confidence.

What is great here is that it will not matter who wears the pants or who does the groceries. In this pairing, there is no need for stereotyping of roles. There is rarely a need for distinct lines of responsibilities to be drawn, and their living arrangement is comfortably undemanding of either party.

They enjoy a genuine mutual respect, so irrespective of whether or not they end up committing to each other over the long term, they continue to be friends and cherish one another. Whether Boar and Tiger come together in love, work or as friends, their relationship will always be characterised by optimism, cheer and decency. Love grows over time and becomes very deep between this pair.

BOAR with RABBIT
Made for each other

Boar and Rabbit make a very happy couple who are extremely well-suited. In fact, they are one of the very best matches in the Chinese Zodiac! There is an enthusiastic approach to life that is both inspiring to watch and also infectious. This pair rings happiness to everyone around them, as their obvious love for each other makes being with them both restful and easy. They are soulmates loving the same things and being motivated by the same kind of people, situations and attainments.

Their aspirations are in line with each other's, so as a couple, it is easy for them to make plans. If they get into a work relationship, they amalgamate their thoughts and efforts very well. Outsiders will find it very difficult to cause friction between them because they have a strong and durable bond.

In 2021, Rabbit's Peach Blossom Energy puts it in the mood for love; and in the arms of the enchanting Boar, it finds plenty of that and more.

While Boar has to contend with the *Loss Star* in its sector, with a Rabbit by its side, all its trials and tribulations become easier to bear. Boar enjoys two

Auspicious Stars from the 24 mountains, but suffers from very weak element luck. So it lacks the energy it needs to effectively capture the opportunities coming its way. But with a Rabbit mate, everything becomes easier. Rabbit gives Boar the confidence and staying power it needs to go after its dreams and aspirations, and as a pair, whatever one aspires after, the other can makes it its dream as well.

> Boar and Rabbit can build a beautiful friendship, and if they fall in love, a very happy and fulfilling family life together. With these two, there is rarely any angst and very little conflict. This is an extremely happy pairing characterised by a quiet elegance.

Neither are clingy or needy types, so they lead very healthy lives alongside the one they share with each other. They do not suffocate each other, yet when they are together, they cannot get enough of one another!

This is a pairing that has the best of everything. Their natural affinity ensures that should they commit themselves to one another, their union will last a long time. This is a wonderful year for Boar and Rabbit in the courting stage to get married, or to take their relationship to the next level. If they find themselves in love, this relationship is worth putting in every effort for.

BOAR with DRAGON
Neither great nor terrible together

While this match may not be the most exciting or dynamic of duos in the Zodiac, it has a good chance of developing into something comfortable that can last. Their temperaments balance well, with Boar's congeniality harmonizing with Dragon's flamboyance. Dragon provides the excitement and adventure in this relationship, while Boar keeps them grounded.

Both are social animals, so they make a wonderfully popular couple in whatever circles they move in. This is a good thing because a Dragon and Boar will need more than just each other to sustain themselves. They play off each other well, but rather better in company than all alone. When left with just each other for company, the cracks begin to appear, and their general kindness towards each other may wear off.

In 2021, this relationship is unlikely to work well, as both have to endure afflictions through the year. Neither will be the strong arms the other will need to be embraced in during times of tribulation.

This coupling works better when everything is peachy. They do not face crises well together, and in times of calamity, one or both could be tempted into the arms of another offering comfort or sympathy. They are not immune to being unfaithful, and when one strays, the other will find it hard to forgive.

If ever there is a case of infidelity, even if these two stay together, the lone incident will be enough to drive a wedge that eventually rips them apart. And 2021 poses just this kind of risk.

In work and business, Dragon and Boar combine well as both are easy-going personalities with a good sense of humour. They laugh their way out of tight spots and neither takes themselves too seriously. But neither will be a particular source of motivation for the other. For that, they have to look elsewhere.

In general, Boar and Dragon get along, if only in lukewarm fashion. They are neither great for each other nor terrible. If their goals align, they can make a good team working towards shared goals, but theirs will never be the kind of relationship to ignite great spark or passion. If either are looking for that in a relationship, they will have to look elsewhere.

BOAR with SNAKE
No good for each other

Boar and Snake are astrological adversaries of the Zodiac, and while they may be attracted to one another in the budding stages of the relationship, it is difficult for this pairing to last into the longer term, and things may get quite unpleasant in the meantime. When they eventually fall out, it is unlikely they can stay friends. Not a recommended match on any level.

Snake is known for being rather selective in its choice of close friends, and most definitely in its search for a mate. The strange thing is that it is easy for Boar and Snake to cross paths and become initially close. Both find the other attractive at the outset, and there will even appear to be much in common. But once they get close, cracks start to appear.

With a Snake, Boar has a knack for saying the wrong thing, always pouring cold water on everything the Snake does. Snake is equally disdainful of what the Boar considers important.

Their attitudes and beliefs do not align at all, and when they clash wits, their fights become quite unpleasant. This is a mismatch of the worst kind, so even though they can be quite close in the early stages of their courtship, in no time at all, their differences are sure to take a toll on their closeness. This is equally the case with friendships as it is with romantic liaisons. Boar and Snake can carry on like they are the best of pals, but when betrayal comes, it comes way below the belt.

Boar and Snake are no good for each other on any level. If they do get married, as they grow older, they will bring out the most negative traits in one another, finding fault and generally causing each other's pessimistic instincts to surface.

They cannot work or live together, so for them to become a couple is definitely not advisable unless there is some kind of bond that can reduce the animosity.

Separately, both Boar and Snake exhibit none of the negative traits they manifest when they are a couple. Their influence on each other is not good, so this match is best avoided. The only way this relationship can work is if one of them has the ascendant of the other in its hour of birth i.e. the Snake born in the hour of the Boar (9pm to 11pm) or the Boar born in the hour of the Snake (9am to 11am).

BOAR with HORSE
An easy-going pairing

While Boar and Horse have no special affinity with one another, they have what it takes to form a loving and lasting relationship with one another. They personify the essence of their respective elements - Fire and Water - being direct opposites in both appearance and personality, with one fast and fiery, and the other slow and steady.

> But put these two together and they can live and work together with great success and happiness. Over time, they develop a special kind of respect for one another's foibles.

Their compatibility arises as much from the good-natured sensitivity of the Boar, who generally is an easy-going person, as from the steadfast loyalty of the Horse. Despite any number of temper tantrums, Boar and Horse always kiss and make up. They do not hold grudges.

In 2021, Horse has better luck than Boar, so it will be Horse that props the both of them up. Boar has the Loss Star, which may manifest in money or other problems; but with a Horse by its side, Boar does not just "survive" the year but positively thrives! The Horse meanwhile finds the Boar a steadying force. Horse goes through a year when it is all systems go, and if left unchecked, could run itself right off the rails. But with a Boar partner, it keeps its feet on the ground.

Horse is a restless, impulsive creature, while Boar tends to be more circumspect and careful, usually thinking things through before acting. Sometimes Boar may be regarded as being too slow and indecisive by the Horse, but they agree to meet halfway and common sense prevails, and so the relationship works well most of the time.

They are comfortable with one another and are generally not too demanding; their interactions are civil, and arguments are rarely allowed to descend into shouting matches. This is a nicely balanced relationship where giving and taking is fairly well-shared between the two.

As business partners, they provide just the right mix of yin and yang to make for a creative and productive partnership. As work colleagues, they are not competitive, so they can become true allies and even good friends. In love and marriage, they make a cozy couple with no fear that one or the other will stray - no passionate fireworks but with excitement enough to sustain a healthy and lasting marriage.

BOAR with SHEEP

Enjoying completion luck together

Boar and Sheep always get along. They are a happy
and compatible couple with plenty of natural affinity.
Whether they have known each other for years or have
only just met, there is an easy camaraderie between
them. Conversation flows freely and they enjoy the
same things. This pair has great and obvious love for
one another and their instinctive congeniality to each
other make them restful and comfortable in one each
other's presence.

In 2021, their relationship gets further
enhanced as their luck stars combine to
form the lucky sum-of-ten. What they
start together, they complete with great
success!

Their natural affinity to each other is infectious,
enabling them to overcome almost anything they face.
As a couple, they win many supporters and friends,
and they will never be short of people wanting to help
them. They make a dynamo team in work matters, and
they build a very happy family life as a married couple.
Both have similar goals and aspirations, and their
attitudes sync up without one having to ever convince
the other over anything.

This year, the Sheep is afflicted by the quarrelsome star, but in the company of the Boar, Sheep's tempers are soothed. Both are amiable personalities, although the Sheep can have a sting, which the Boar successfully neutralises every time.

Boar and Sheep make up two thirds of the group of allies described as the Diplomats of the Zodiac. They share gentle dispositions, and their lifestyles mirror their desire for a quiet and elegant existence. When these two get together, you can be assured they know how to enjoy life. In fact, they will hone each other's expensive tastes in food, wine, holidays and experiences.

But Boar and Sheep are disciplined individuals who will put in the work without a fuss if they need to make the money. Not for these two making money for money's sake. No, for them, they will likely spend a large proportion of what they earn.

This year promises love, passion and desires fulfilled for Boar and Sheep couples who are married. Their luck holds strong and affect both positively. Sheep has stronger element luck than Boar, so Sheep will be the one driving this relationship in 2021. But whichever of the two is in charge does not matter, because the other will happily give its full support.

BOAR with MONKEY

Loving life together in 2021

When Boar and Monkey get together, there is always a ton of life and laughter. These two outgoing personalities have a lot of natural affinity and the coming year brings even more. Their luck patterns in 2021 combine to form the auspicious sum-of-ten, which indicates they are successful when they work together on anything, and when they communicate, there is always plenty of stimulating dialogue.

> Boar and Monkey are always considered a great fit. Their attitudes towards life may be different, but they are complementary.

What the Monkey does really well, the Boar has no interest in developing. And vice versa. There is never any rivalry between a Boar and Monkey. As a team, they each find their own way to contribute without stepping onto each other's turf. This couple is motivated by different things, yet they often build a wonderful co-existence. The security each feels when with the other allows them to be totally themselves. Before they even build a home and family together, it could already feel like they are a long-married couple. Their easy familiarity makes this a cozy compatibility - a recipe for a long-lasting marriage or relationship.

For Boar and Monkey, things look extremely rosy this year, especially with their excellent joint luck indications. Individually, Monkey is much stronger than Boar in terms of element luck, but Monkey benefits from Boar's Big and Small Auspicious from the 24 Mountains. Successes come easily to both when they pair up.

As a married couple, they are so compatible and easy-going that even the tiniest things can make them happy. They are the kind of couple to celebrate every little thing. From birthdays to anniversaries to hallmark holidays, these two find every reason to throw a party. They are highly social animals so they make excellent hosts. And because they both enjoy the company of others, you will often find Boar-Monkey couples becoming a fixture on the local social scene.

Both enjoy the good life. Neither is stingy in the least, so you won't get one nagging the other over household or joint expenditures. Their affinity grows as the year unfolds, and their indulgence for each other's whims only strengthen their commitment to each other. This is a pair who will be held as a shining example of matrimonial bliss.

BOAR with ROOSTER

Boar is happy to let Rooster take charge

The relationship between Boar and Rooster is one of great expectations. Here Rooster accepts Boar's languid view of the world and can even identify with Boar's love of luxury and the good life. However, Rooster should be the breadwinner, being better at making money, handling it and making sure the domestic budget balances.

Boar is more than happy to let Rooster take charge as long as there is enough to indulge in the good things in life.

When Boar and Rooster get together, Boar gives Rooster a totally free hand to make all the money, initiate all the projects and negotiate all the deals, with no questions asked. In fact, Rooster will be left in charge all the way. But because Boar is so congenial and loving always, Rooster will never mind. Boar contributes in other ways, and this helps rather than hinders this relationship.

In 2021, the vitality of the Rooster is exceptional. It is a very good year for the Rooster, and this helps this couple indulge themselves to the limit. The attitude of these two towards life may be different, but they are definitely complementary.

The good thing is that Boar knows a good thing when it sees one, and having caught a Rooster, is unlikely to let it go. Boar is thus always tolerant, and whatever criticisms are levelled its way are simply ignored. Boar is clever and pragmatic in this respect and does not allow mere words to get in the way of a good relationship. They make a good couple as Rooster is more than happy to go along with Boar's social ambitions. As a result, they can be extremely happy together.

In 2021, the energy levels of Rooster and Boar are at two extreme ends of the scale. Rooster is all systems go; its attitude through the year is one of enthusiasm and great vitality. Boar on the other hand is hit by the lows coupled with the Loss Star. The cosmic forces of the year seem to be absorbing all of Boar's energies, but Boar enjoys both Big and Small Auspicious, indicating pockets of great good fortune during the year.

With a Rooster partner, Boar's fortunes get enhanced as Rooster's go-getting attitude and fabulous element luck this year will ensure the opportunities that come to them as a couple do not slip away.

BOAR with DOG

Soulmates weathering a difficult year

These two share the Zodiac House of Domesticity together, which spells good things for this pair. Belonging to the same house gives them exceptional affinity, so whatever they get up to brings them a great deal of happiness. But 2021 could see some problems.

In 2021, Boar and Dog are both afflicted by the Betrayal Star, which causes all kinds of arguments to take place and even for dishonesty to creep into the picture.

In view of this, Boar or Dog, or both, could lose interest in the relationship. Having the Betrayal Star brings hard times, so if there are problems between them this year, they must remember that underlying all the negativity, there is genuine caring for each other.

Boar knows that very few things cause Dog to lose sight of what makes existence meaningful. But the Dog does have a tendency to preach, occasionally getting on its high horse to lecture those close to it about anything and everything. Boar cannot take this and eventually starts to see the Dog as a tiresome nag! When things get too tiresome, Boar could very well trot off into the sunset.

This is not a bad relationship and these two enjoy a genuine mutual love, but Dog and Boar are not insanely passionate about each other. There is instead a lovely warmth between them - and thus it is important that this coziness does not get shattered by too much nagging and lecturing.

In the event of a rift, note that Dog and Boar are two of the Zodiac's signs who dislike noisy quarrels, so in this year of trials and tribulations, it is possible both could simply throw their hands up in the air and leave it to the passage of time to clear the energies.

Dog benefits from Boar's philosophy of cest la vie, adopting a carefree attitude towards life in general and opting to cope with whatever comes in a relaxed manner. But there is sincerity in this pairing and both are genuinely agreeable. Boar does not judge the Dog, and it is good for Dog to reciprocate in a similar manner.

In no time at all, the year with all its discordant chi will be over. But while living through it, Dog will take great comfort in having someone like the Boar to lean on. It is just important for both sides to appreciate the special affinity they both have, and not allow anything to spoil their great potential.

BOAR with BOAR

Confrontational vibes in 2021

A coming together of two Boars is not exactly the perfect match, although it can work in some years. This however is not the case in 2021 when both are hit by the Betrayal Star. Two Boars in 2021 see a couple of normally happy-go-lucky individuals constantly going for each other's throats.

The thing about the coming together of two people belonging to the same Boar sign is their overt possessiveness and inherent jealousy. They can become so neurotic about each other's faults, even when they should stand by one another. They afford other signs that extra patience, but alas, not each other.

Somehow two Boars can be rather unkind about one another's eccentricities, taking delight in pointing out faults each time an opportunity arises.

This unfortunately reflects their warped attitude towards their own sign, because normally, the Boar is neither disagreeable nor critical of others. But two Boars together can elicit some anti-social and mutually disagreeable behaviour. It is the greatest of pairings, and definitely one to avoid in 2021. The coming year sees them wary of one another, and they will possess divergent interests. Neither will support the other, and when they go headlong at each other, disagreements easily degenerate into extremely confrontational behaviour.

> In 2021, Boar's energy levels are very weak.
> When it gets together with another of its sign, the constant jibes and sniping leaves them weaker still. This results in a mutual shortage of good yang chi, leaving not enough time to recuperate to gain back the strength and inclination to be cordial. Not a good pairing this year as the feelings that arise are simply so negative.

There is a lack of patience and little or no chemistry between them. As soon as something goes wrong, the finger pointing begins, so in this year when the shadow of the #7 looms large, two Boar do tend to bring out the worst ineach other.

Under better times, two Boars can get along; but in 2021, they spell bad news together. In the long run, this is not the best of partnerships. Two Boars are merely average together in good times, and terrible in bad times. They can never inspire each other to great heights, and with the lack of any great passion, there is little to suggest this pair would be good together.

Boar's Monthly
Horoscope 2021
Chapter 6

Adjust your expectations and don't be in a hurry for results

The Boar does not face an easy year in 2021. Your element luck is weak, which dampens your spirits and saps you of energy to carry on when things get tough. What the Boar needs to do is to fight the urge to give up when problems arise. Change your mindset to look on dilemmas as challenges that will only make you stronger. You have good friends in your midst. Don't be averse to calling on them for help when you need. If you talk about your problems, they no longer seem insurmountable, and solutions can be found. Not a year to go after anything too risky or ambitious, but have a quiet eye to the future when things look more promising. A year to learn to enjoy the simpler pleasures of life.

1st Month
February 4th - March 5th 2021

....

FOLLOW YOUR INSTINCTS

This looks to be a quiet year of steady building, and things start off very well. In this first month of the Ox year, you enjoy the arrival of the *Heaven Star*, which blesses you with good judgement and instincts. What this means is that you do not need to seek the opinion of so many people when making important decisions. Listen and trust your inner voice instead. The #6 star brings you good mentor luck. If there is someone in a position to help you, seek them out. A productive time for young Boars making their way in life. This is a month to go with the flow and take things as they come. Even if things do not go completely according to plan, trust that everything will work out. Do not fight against the current.

....

Work & Career - *Some irritating rivals*

You feel glad to be working and the office seems a joy, but there is some gossip aimed at you. Your best move is to ignore it. You have the support of the bosses so there is nothing to worry about. If you react by lashing back, you merely invite more of the same. Build your own network of allies at the workplace. It will quickly be obvious who are for and who are against you. If you play your cards right, there is nothing your rivals can do to harm you. While they may cause some temporary irritation or mental stress, they are unable to hurt you in any significant way. For protection, it is a good idea to carry the **Kuan Kung on Horseback Anti-Betrayal Amulet**.

> A mentor gives you a significant leg up. There may be those jealous of you, but they can do little to harm you. Do however stay aware who your friends and who your enemies are.

Business - *Good time for entrepreneurs*

Good opportunities open up for deal making. New ideas can be put into motion successfully and quickly. You have some important patrons who can join up and bring their vital contacts with them. Family members can also invest in your business. If you are your own boss and make your own decisions then it is best, as there can some misunderstandings between partners. Try to resolve issues as soon as they arise before they get bigger. If not, agree to disagree till both sides can come to an amicable solution. If you can compromise, you can achieve a lot. Life is easier for those who can say yes or no without having to check with a counter-balancing force.

Love & Relationships - *Luck in love*

A great time for Boars looking for love! Also a
lucky period to get engaged or married. If in a new
relationship, now augurs well to declare your feelings
as they are likely to be reciprocated. With heavenly luck
shining down on you, only nice things occur on the love
front. More so when you are interested in the long run
rather than with short term flings. Another possibility is
for something romantic to evolve from what has always
been a platonic relationship. If this happens, it will be a
happy surprise for everyone including yourself!

Home & Family - *Feeling broody*

Your family fulfils you in many ways. There is lots
happening on the home front. If you have young
children, this will be an extremely fulfilling time. Your
love of parenting becomes pronounced, which means
those who are the recipients benefit tremendously.
Couples without children may get broody, so a good
solution is to surround yourself with nephews and
nieces who can allow your parental instincts to flourish.

School & Education - *Mentor luck*

Studies go well for the young Boar. If you have been
doing well in your studies, this will spur you onto
greater heights. Things go infinitely better if you have
a strong mentor figure in your life. Get to know your
teachers better, you have a lot to learn from them. A
time when you can make some really good new friends.

2nd Month
March 6th - April 4th 2021

....

MISFORTUNE STAR. STAY RESILIENT.

Not the easiest of months, as the *Five Yellow* misfortune star makes an apperance. This causes all kinds of obstacles to arise, making life a series of stops and starts. A big part of how the month pans out will depend on your attitude. Choose to look at the positive side of everything and learn to laugh when things don't go according to plan. Everything happens for a reason and this month you have to trust that idiom. Having said that, better to stay low key and to remain risk averse. Don't invest in the stock market, don't assume a high profile, don't give others a reason to envy you. No need to claim credit even for work due to you. The more generous-hearted you are, the better your karmic benefits.

....

Work & Career - *Office politics*

Another gossipy month where you may get idle talk and politicking that can take on dangerous dimensions if out of control. You are bound to be affected even if you stay above the fray; and this month the stars are not in your favour. Try not to take sides or be too critical. When you give your two cents' worth of opinion, you are also opening yourself to criticism and being misquoted. Certain things you say may be taken out of context or worse, intentionally twisted to put you in a bad light. Best to stay tight lipped. No need to share your opinions unless absolutely necessary.

Even if your boss loses his cool, you must stay calm as two wrongs do not make a right. Things improve next month, so cheer up.

Business - *Stay low profile*

Not the most profitable month. Money losses are possible and there seems to be risks afoot. There are potholes to manoeuvre and even if you fall in one or two, as long as you can crawl out, consider yourself lucky. Inaction is the best action! Anything that attracts attention may be accompanied by bad or unfortunate events. Avoid publicity. Don't sign new deals or hold any launches attended by the media. If such events are already planned, delegate someone else to be spokesperson. Best if you stay in the background. Stick to the familiar. Do not venture into unchartered territory. Make all important decisions next month when your luck improves. Even if you are pressed against the wall, resist big commitments, as you will regret doing anything momentous now and may lose money in the process. Since things are stacked against you, this may be a good time to go on vacation!

Love & Relationships - *Avoid love triangles*

Little passion when it comes to your love life but it is probably best that way. To pursue an overly active love affair now may backfire and make you miserable. Avoid love triangles as they will not end well. Stay legitimate. If there is no-one suitable on the horizon, find other interests. Not the best time to begin a new relationship. Married Boars may suffer misunderstandings with their spouse, so try to be more understanding.

Education - *Lacklustre*

You suffer from a severe shortage of energy and things seem unattractive and dull. There is lots of work and you feel like you cannot cope. Falling ill from the flu or some sports-related injury can make matters worse by slowing you down at a time when you are already feeling weak. If you cannot finish your assignments on time, you may have to sacrifice some leisure activities to keep on top of the game.

CURE FOR THE MONTH: A good idea to carry the **Five Element Pagoda Amulet** at all times throughout this month. The *Five Yellow* wreaks all kind of havoc, but having this amulet with you shields you from the worst of its effects.

3rd Month
April 5th - May 5th 2021

....

RELATIONSHIPS IMPROVE. PROMISING ROMANCE LUCK.

Your luck improves and you are on an upcycle. The romance star makes an appearance. If single and hoping to find true love, you could meet the match of your dreams! Paying special attention to your love life now could land you someone you can truly consider a soulmate. Remember, if looking for a relationship that goes beyond the superficial, you have to play your part. Don't let peer pressure or the need to conform limit who you date or who you give attention to. If you widen your horizons, you could find yourself someone very special indeed! A month where relationships go well, making this a good time to expand your network, deepen your friendships and mend relationships that need work.

....

Work & Career - *New skills*

A month when you get along with everyone, making it a pleasant time all round. This includes the time you spend at the office. Those yet to make real friends at work could find yourself clicking with certain colleagues beyond just work. Your communicative skills are at their height and you feel like sharing. A productive month when it comes to accumulation of knowledge and the acquiring of skills. You continue to learn new things on the job, but if you make a concerted effort to formalise that learning through study, research and formal courses, the rewards can be magnificent. A month when you push the envelope and surpass plateaus you may have felt stuck on for a while.

Embrace new ideas and new ways of doing things. A time when you can expand your skill set considerably.

Business - *Powers of persuasion*

Good month for holding important meetings, launching new products, closing deals and interacting with the media. You are persuasive and what you say works brilliantly with your audience. Your ability to steer others over to your point of view is impressive, and you tend to have the upper hand in any negotiation. Your biggest asset now is your diplomacy, and your skill is with coming up with ideas then convincing everyone else they had a hand in it too. Continue along this vein and you can make plenty happen just the way you wish. Sales improve and problems that plagued you before become a distant memory. Money luck is promising and new income streams result from networking efforts on your part. You have that rare luck of attracting the right kind of people into your orbit, whether as team member, partner or client.

Love & Relationships - *Delightful*

A delightful time filled with everything you are searching for. You're feeling confident and positive, and this attracts you many admirers. If single, you will have no shortage of suitors. But if you want to end up with the right one, don't be in a rush to get locked into a steady relationship. Enjoy the romancing! Married Boars however need to beware the influence of the *External Romance Star*. Interested third parties may have designs on you, and if not careful, they could sweep you off your feet and cause you to do something you regret.

Education - *Juggling everything nicely*

A great time for the young Boar. Everything is going swell. Your friendship circles bring you joy and you're staying on top of your studies. Once you get onto an upward spiral, the sky's the limit. Keep working hard and keep enjoying life!

ENHANCER FOR THE MONTH:
Carry the **Windhorse Success Amulet** to give success luck a boost. A month when everything is going right for you, one in which your *Big Auspicious* luck could ripen!

4th Month
May 6th - June 5th 2021

FEELING ARGUMENTATIVE, BUT MORE PRODUCTIVE AT WORK

The Boar has the *Quarrelsome Star* to contend with, but lucky you as it combines with the #7 to form the auspicious *Sum-of-Ten*. This suggests that despite misunderstandings, things work out nicely in the end. You remain productive and your ideas continue to hold weight and bear fruit. No matter whether others can get along with you or not, you remain valuable for what you bring to the table. Don't however take that for granted. Push someone beyond their limit and anyone is replaceable, including you at your utmost best. Stay charming and diplomatic despite your occasional bad temper or irritable outbursts.

Work & Career - *Working on your own*

Not the time to try to get ahead at work. Continue being productive but don't lock horns with anybody. You are more quarrelsome than usual and you may find working with others especially tough this month. Avoid too much collaborative work. If you can engineer assignments that you can tackle on your own, things go much more smoothly. You have too many good ideas that others don't agree with and sharing them only leads to frustration. Don't try to argue your point. Save your breath for a time when your speech is more convincing. While energetic and keen to contribute, keeping a low profile is your best strategy now. Saying too much could lead to you saying the wrong thing, creating the wrong impression.

Others may vex you, but try not to react. Don't voice your feelings so readily, as those feelings may change.

Business - Bureaucracy

Bureaucracy slows down the course of doing business. This gets on your nerves but making a fuss only makes things worse. Some things are out of your control and a bad attitude won't get you on the right side of the powers that be. There are delays which seem unavoidable, you just have to live with it. Keep frustrations to yourself, as the less people know your feelings, the better. Not a good time to venture into new partnerships or projects. Instead, focus on what you are already doing. Support existing staff that show promise. Promote them to new levels if you see fit. Be careful when it comes to communicating anything, as there are risks to conveying things the wrong way. If you need to negotiate, it may be better to send someone you trust than do it personally. You have good luck now, but not in the communications department.

Love & Relationships - *Drama*

Love is not smooth sailing and there could be drama in your love life. Things could get loud, especially for those who have been in a relationship a long time. If you fight, agree to disagree before one of you says something you cannot take back. Don't insist on having the last word - this will make matters so much worse. Young love birds enjoy the month better, but if not yet in a formal relationship, better wait till next month to declare your feelings.

Home & Family - *Recluse*

Your people skills are at a low ebb and a hermit's life suddenly seems pleasant. You are not so suave with your words, so the less said the better. Indeed, it is better to stay home and enjoy its quiet pleasures than suffer from verbal diarrhea in public!

Education - *Feeling grumpy*

Your disposition borders on sulkiness and others may not like you for it. Your grumpiness could alienate friends who think you are uncooperative. In turn, they get on your nerves too so there is little love lost. If you can't help but fight, best to use the month for alone time or self-study.

CURE FOR THE MONTH: The Boar benefits from carrying the **Apple Peace Amulet** this month.

5th Month
June 6th - July 6th 2021

ILLNESS STAR SAPS YOUR ENERGY, BUT YOU ENJOY WEALTH LUCK

You feel under the weather more often than usual. Or you have so much on your plate you just don't have enough hours in a day! But despite a poorer physical disposition, mentally you are sharp as ever. Those in business have plenty of new ideas and getting these off the ground is both easy and effective. You meet the right people and are surrounded by the right generals. If you can get your team to work cohesively as one entity, you get more done while having to do less. Focus on management. Don't try to do everything yourself. Get enough sleep and take care of your health. Learn to trust others. As a boss, don't micromanage. As a parent, don't helicopter parent.

Work & Career - *Beware overwork*

You are loaded with work which you can normally handle, but this month, completing your tasks becomes harder and more arduous. Your health takes a hit and falling sick when you have work worries is no fun! Delegate work where possible; get others involved and don't try to do everything yourself. Ask for help if you need; you can repay favours later. Strategy-wise, this might be a good thing, as asking colleagues to help will strengthen your relationships. Don't overwork as you may get so exhausted you make mistakes. It is easy to keep surviving on endless coffee and not realize you are burning out till you find out you have no more wick left to burn.

Physically and mentally, you are prone to exhaustion. If work is piling up, do something. Don't just soldier on.

Business - *Fierce rivals*

There is promise of big wealth but it does not come easy. Business now will be about beating the competition. Rivals appear out of nowhere, and some will play dirty. You need to react quickly to keep your customers. Time doing PR will be time well spent. Think of new ways to market your product but try not to incur heavy capital outlays as cash flow may be tight. Be open to ideas proposed to you. Something big could come along, as the month star combines with the year star to give you the *Big Wealth Ho Tu*.

ENHANCER OF THE MONTH:
Have the **Ho Tu Enhancer** near you at all times to bring out the positive aspects of the month for you.

Love & Relationships - *Heating up*
If your personal life has been quiet, this month may see things heating up again. You are in the mood for love! Singles have no problem finding partners but if looking for that someone special, it pays to be more discerning. One-on-one dates could lead you to become closer than you'd like to a particular someone. For married Boars, a good time to take a holiday together.

Health & Safety - *Be more careful*
Your health is poorly but keeping active is a good way to fight off the illness blues. Feeling sorry for yourself will only prolong whatever ailment you think you have. Having said that, be more careful and don't take your health for granted. If you know something's not right, head for a check-up just for some peace of mind. You are more accident prone, so watch where you're stepping. Careless falls could put you out of action longer than you'd like and mess up some of your best laid plans.

Education - *Avoid dangerous sports*
You are not in top form so avoid dangerous sports since you are prone to injuries. If part of your curriculum, avoid taking risks on the pitch. It always pays to be careful when one has the accident star hovering.

6th Month
July 7th - Aug 7th 2021

SOME WELCOME CHANGES IN YOUR LIFE

A glorious month of breakthroughs when things you've been working on finally come together. A time when you have solid results to show for your hard work. Take time to savour your accomplishments rather than simply motoring on. For some, this will be a month of realizations. You summon up the conviction to make some major changes you've been contemplating. Other changes happen of their own accord, but all for the better. While the Boar is going through an average year, you have pockets of fabulous good fortune, and this month could see some of that materializing for you. An exciting new chapter of your life may be unfolding!

Work & Career - *Opportunities to shine*
A challenging time at work but one that provides many memorable moments! You can barely keep track of what's happening as new staff appear, old ones get transferred and new projects get installed. You may even be posted to a different department or given new tasks. If you feel out of sync, don't worry as you

quickly fall into step with your new responsibilities. You are in your element and full of confidence. Keep a positive mindset and you are halfway there. Impressing colleagues and superiors is easy since you have many opportunities to shine. You make yourself noticeable in a good way and others appreciate your presence. You also possess admirable leadership qualities, for which you may be handsomely rewarded.

If dedicated, you may be promoted or given a position of greater importance.

Business - *Impressive leadership*

You find yourself more involved than ever in day-to-day operations. Put your stamp of authority at work and get involved. Your leadership and people skills make it easy for you to inspire your staff. The more persevering you stay, the better you benefit. Keep the big picture in mind when making plans. This is a time of big changes whether at work or industry wide. Keep abreast of everything in order to make good decisions. Maintain your perspective and there is no difficulty triumphing over the competition. Some may experience a newly discovered sixth sense - listen to that inner voice when making decisions; it will help you. No need to consult with too many people in every decision you make. Carry the **Lunar Mansion Talisman** to help you get your timing right on your decisions and actions.

Black Tortoise
Talisman

Love & Relationships - *Be impulsive*

A short vacation with your spouse will do you both a world of good. A new environment where neither are stressed out by the pressures of work is just what you may need to reignite any spark that may have dimmed in the tedium of everyday living. If part of a tired twosome, book your dream holiday and whisk your loved one away somewhere exotic! Don't spend too much time deliberating, or you'll end up not going. Be impulsive!

Home & Family - *Nesting instincts*

Your strong nesting instinct may pull you in two directions, between work and home. While previously you were happy to work late or earn overtime, you now prefer to rush home for more family time. This is the right course as personal contentment and making your loved ones happy becomes more important than status and wealth, and will end up getting you further.

Education - *New challenges*

A good time to try new things. Nothing is set in stone and you enjoy the flexibility of change. Seek guidance from teachers and adults you respect. Schoolwork goes well and you score high grades. You do well even in subjects you were never strong in, so you should be pleased with your progress. You have good potential to demonstrate leadership, so if there are positions open, apply!

7th Month
Aug 8th - Sept 7th 2021

A BRUTAL TIME. TEMPER YOUR EXPECTATIONS.

Your run of good luck gets temporarily halted with the arrival of the #9 star. The energies of loss get magnified, making this a time to be extra careful. Do not risk money on precarious investments. Avoid gambling. Don't attract attention to yourself. Even when you experience good fortune, stay low key. Those envious of your success could do you harm. There is betrayal in the air, and the sad thing is it may not even be intentional. Be understanding but do not be trusting. Watch who you let into your inner circle. When seeking advice, keep in mind the other person could have a hidden agenda. At times like this, it is best to rely on yourself than to depend too much on others.

Work & Career - *Take back control*

A competitive environment at work may drain you of energy. It seems all eyes are on you and when you slip up, there is someone to show they can do the job better. Constantly having to prove your worth can become tiring and stressful. Don't allow yourself to get sucked into that game. You can do your job, and you know what you can achieve and at what pace. Work harder but don't let others pressure you into delivering impossible deadlines, causing you to make mistakes in the process. At the end of the day, you're the one that has to shoulder the responsibility if things go wrong. Take back control. There is no need to be so accommodating.

It is human nature to take down the competition. But if you're going to retaliate, retaliate smart!

Business - *Disputes over money*
There may be disputes over money matters as you discover some glaring discrepancies in the accounts. It gets worse if it involves one or more partners, as everyone passes the buck and ducks the blame. Even before the clouds clear, other partners may not see eye-to-eye with you. Problems intensify if a third party enters the picture. Your own decisions are more valuable than checking with others who may have their own agendas. They either give bad advice or worse, trick you with false data.

Brainstorming is not worth the time spent, so stick to your own guns. Continue doing what you are good at. Limit contact with those you feel uncomfortable working with. Better to err on the side of caution, even if it means potential loss of revenue. Your wealth luck is currently weak, so you already stand to lose money. Just don't take risks that are unnecessary.

Love & Relationships - *Troublemakers*

You're not in the mood for love, and your partner could be feeling the apparent neglect. Don't get into trivial fights over this. If there's anything weighing on your mind, share with your partner. Doing so will lift a load off your shoulders and make you natural allies over a common enemy. This could do wonders for your relationship, just what you need when feeling weary dealing with a cutthroat world. Beware third parties trying to come between you and your spouse. If someone undermines your partner, there is no need to show them any courtesy. It is more important to keep your marriage strong.

Education - *Rebel with a cause*

You are feeling rebellious, wanting to break free from routine and do your own thing. You are at the height of adolescence when beginning to experience independence, and this month you are tempted to take this freedom to a daring new level. But keep an eye on your responsibilities. There is nothing cooler than a responsible "wild child" who continues to deliver on grades.

CURE FOR THE MONTH: This month you need the **Anti-Robbery Amulet** to temper the Loss Star in your chart. Carry at all times.

8th Month
Sept 8th - Oct 7th 2021

WEALTH STAR BRINGS GOOD FORTUNE. BIG AUSPICIOUS RIPENS?

The *Star of Current Prosperity* arrives, bringing wealth and strengthening every other kind of luck also. You are feeling strong, making it easy to weather difficulties that crop up. While there may be challenges ahead, the way you view them transforms them into great opportunities. Whatever your aspirations, this month you can dream big and start taking definite steps to fulfilling those dreams. Verbalise what you are striving for. Don't be scared to tell people what you're hoping to achieve in the mistaken belief they will laugh, talk you down or steal your idea. The more you share, the clearer your goals become in your mind, and the more likely you will be to achieve them.

Work & Career - *Promotion luck*

A fabulous month all round! Everybody sings your praises and a promotion is a sniff away. Even if your rise in rank is not quite formalized, accept any added responsibilities with open arms, as they signal good things to come in the near future! You are about to become a lot more important at work, so don't mess

things up by getting idle! Income luck is ticking over
nicely so you are unlikely to be short of cash unless you
are the extravagant type. Don't get greedy grasping
for perks and pay raises; you will be justly rewarded.
Be patient! You could even be offered a partnership
or stock options. Whatever the guise, good things are
headed your way!

> *Those great new ideas you've had in
> your head can now be put forward
> without danger of them being stolen or
> brushed aside.*

Business - *Great new opportunities*

Opportunities abound! You could meet someone who
proposes some lucrative deal. Or a casual chat with
someone you barely know can lead to some big project.
Whatever the case, such encounters bring huge benefits
which may not be immediately apparent. A month to
keep your eyes peeled! No idea is too big to pursue.
And don't rule out opportunities unrelated to your
main line of work; there could be a goldmine waiting to
be tapped! A highly productive time which is especially
satisfying because the rewards are not just monetary;
they bring pride and personal satisfaction as well.
Those of you who are happiest will be those doing what
they're doing not just for the money. Look beyond the
numbers when gauging "success".

Love & Relationships - *Love in the air!*

Love is in the air and you have no shortage of suitors to sweep you off your feet. But there could be a special someone you've been admiring. Be bold with your feelings. Don't hold back. A month when true love can blossom and it will not matter how long you have known each other. Go with your heart. Don't make yourself tick too many boxes. The right person on paper could be very incompatible with you in real life. And vice versa.

Home & Family - *Recharge*

Don't forget to relax even if very busy at work. Let your body recharge so you can fully deal with all responsibilities at the start of each week. Others are likely to find you more charming hence more fun to do deals with if you're well rested with a good sense of humour.

Education - *Enjoying your school*

You absorb knowledge easily, and concepts you found tricky before suddenly click. You enjoy the attention of your teachers, and one or two could become real mentor figures.

ENHANCER FOR THE MONTH: Carry the **Asset Wealth Bull Amulet** so that the money you make now lasts! This capitalises on your Prosperity Star ensuring the new cash you make contributes to your expanding net worth!

9th Month
Oct 8th - Nov 6th 2021

A MONTH TO BE CAREFUL.

The stars align making the resident annual loss star doubly perilous. The #7 star is not to be taken lightly so the advice is to lie low. Avoid taking risks and extricate yourself from any argument or altercation you find yourself in. Conflicts don't end well, so work at mitigating them before they become something big. Don't let pride get the better of you. Survive to fight another day. There will be disappointments to weather and betrayals to contend with, but put it down to the unfriendly energies and perhaps you won't feel so bad. Accept small losses and be careful if involved in business. Make sure you are not exposed as you are vulnerable and could lose big money.

Work & Career - *Lie low*

Work life may be unpredictable. There could be conflicting feelings where your career path is concerned. Misunderstandings make you want to throw your hands up in the air and quit; but this is not a good time to make reckless decisions that could have a serious impact on your future. Wearing the **colours blue and black** will help quell the destructive stars in your cycle. You have a lot of destructive Metal energy in your chart now, so wearing Water colours engages element therapy which weakens its negative influences. Things improve next month. For now, lie low and don't draw too much attention to yourself.

> Beware enemies in the ranks who may plot against you. Best to know who your friends and allies are, but the lines may get blurred this month.

Business - *Play it safe*

Beware of getting cheated or conned! Your ambitions to get rich may land you in hot water if you too readily fall for scams. There is unfortunately no easy money to be made now. In fact, quite the opposite; it is easy to lose money, so avoid taking financial risks, and beware working with entities you do not know well. Avoid giving credit, no risky investments, don't speculate on the stock market, conserve your capital. This month is best spent quietly and not making any major moves. Even if things may not be working out as you want, making big changes or shuffling people around could land you with an even bigger disaster on your hands. Keep an eagle eye on your internal, personal affairs. You could be cheated even by those you consider "your own people".

Love & Relationships - *Don't get too serious*

Things may get complicated in your love life. You are prone to arguments and some of you could suffer serious fallings out with your partner or spouse. Give each other space. Don't insist on finishing a quarrel because there will be no winners. Don't get too clingy or this could repel your other half. Single Boars have little luck when it comes to dating. You're more emotional than usual, a far cry from your usual, charming self. Unless you find just the right foil for your prickly personality, first dates may not lead to second dates. Don't move too fast and keep things casual. You don't want to spoil your chances for when your luck is better.

Education - *Average*

A fairly average month for the young Boar in school. It may be more difficult to achieve the results you are used to, but everyone has good and bad days. Don't be too hard on yourself. Keep up your consistency by ensuring you get your homework done before taking time out to relax.

CURE FOR THE MONTH: Carry the **Anti Betrayal Amulet** to guard against allies turning into enemies. Female Boars should carry the **Nightspot Protection Amulet** if you go out alone at night.

10th Month
Nov 7th - Dec 6th 2021

HEAVEN LUCK HELPS YOU ALONG. THINGS FALLING INTO PLACE.

A good month for the Boar, much better than last month when you felt like some sort of punching bag. The *Heaven Star* pays a visit, bringing blessings of all kinds. You patch things up with friends whom you may have temporarily fallen out with. Work life goes a lot better and you find yourself with a bevy of allies. There are many who want to help you, and when they offer their help, accept gracefully. Even if you feel you do not need assistance, no harm displaying gratitude. This kind of mindset will win you friends, some who become especially important as time goes by. A good month for networking, diversifying your social circle and building up a solid friendship base.

Work & Career - *Get involved*

You enjoy solid support with accolades being piled on so relentlessly you may feel quite embarassed! Enjoy the attention but don't get too big for your boots. There is no need however to be overly self-deprecating either, as it is not every day that you get so well praised. Use this time to take positive strides forward. Offer to do more. Volunteer for more responsibilities even if not part of your regular job scope. Get involved in more projects. The more you do, the more efficient you get. And the more sections of the company you are involved in, the easier each individual task becomes. Everything is interconnected and when you are involved in multiple aspects, you enjoy a wonderful bird's eye view, giving you a distinct advantage over your colleagues and peers.

Your people skills are thriving making this an opportune time to expand your network of social and professional contacts.

Business - *Collaborations*

Fortune favours the bold and the Boar is full of *gung-ho* energy now. Others get energized by your attitude, giving you a natural mantle to lead. Those heading a team or your own organization find it easy to motivate those you lead, and when you set your mind to it, you multiply your productivity manifold. Tap your network of friends and acquaintances. When you collaborate, new opportunities open up for you. A month when it serves you well to try everything. You can afford to take risks, both with time and money. If asked for a favour, grant it if it does not inconvenience you too much - it will be more than repaid later. Wealth luck is promising so you can approach new investments with confidence.

A good time to expand, diversify and move up a level.

Love & Relationships - *Romantic*

A delightfully romantic month! A good time for reconnecting and rediscovering the joys of what you and your partner have in common. Do things together and pull yourself out of the monotony of everyday living. Take a holiday if that's what you need. For the single Boar, there are many opportunities for intense passion. Those hoping to find that someone special may just do that. Don't let peer pressure influence you in your taste when it comes to whom you should be with, or you could sabotage your own chances of finding a true soul mate.

Education - *Doing well*

The more you do, the happier and more satisfied you become. You earn the admiration and commendation of your teachers and are popular with your peers. Your good mood propels you onto an upward spiral, helping you shine in both schoolwork and in your social life. Keep up your positive spirit to ensure this winning streak lasts!

ENHANCER FOR THE MONTH: You benefit greatly from carrying the **Dragon Heavenly Seal Amulet**. This awakens the Heaven Star in your chart to bring you all that your heart desires.

11th Month
Dec 7th - Jan 5th 2022

OBSTACLES ARISE & MISUNDERSTANDINGS ABOUND

The *Five Yellow* brings all kinds of problems. Nothing you do seems to go right, and even doing nothing will not save you from disapproval and peer pressure. Being an unlucky month, it is filled with more downs than ups, so extreme care is needed to emerge unscathed. Lying low is the best choice as to do nothing is better than tempting fate. Big projects involving higher risks are out of the question. Any events that concern money should be put off to another time. If postponement is not possible, delegate the tasks, as to take them on will stress you out and they may not go as planned. Accidents are on the cards so be extra careful, even if over small matters, as it is much better to be safe than sorry. You may encounter bad news, so brace yourself if such an eventuality occurs.

Work & Career - *Avoid the unfamiliar*

There are potholes to navigate at work. While last month you could do no wrong, this month is quite the opposite. It seems the easiest thing in the world to make mistake after mistake. Particularly when you try too hard. Be a performing member of your organization but don't try to be the star. Avoid anything too unfamiliar or risky. Remember whatever you do and know best may not even work out let alone things out of your league. Do your job as well as you can, but don't try to take on more than you can chew.

Resist the urge to take on too much. This is a month to lie low.

Business - *Obstacles*

Many things are troubling you, so you are not performing at your best. Try to clear the most important issues first and leave the niggling ones for later. You are human and cannot cope with excessive tension. Stay on top of things or you could find rival undermining what you have achieved so far. Keep a sharp eye and ear on what is going on around you or you may miss some vital information. This is quite difficult as you tend to focus on trivial matters but try to concentrate on things and people that have a direct influence on your business. You may encounter obstacles but though they seem overwhelming, do not worry as they will fade over time.

Love & Relationships - *Stay upbeat*
Staying put and being where you are now is better than trying to take your relationship to the next level. Be thankful nothing is going wrong. If you've been allowing certain hang-ups to worry you, now is the time to get rid of them. These worrisome thoughts can only hamper what can be a loving relationship. Be supportive of your partner. Your mood rubs off, so try to maintain a cheerful disposition even if things are dragging you down. For singles, save looking for love for another time.

Home & Family - *Refuge*
Your home is your refuge so when things seem to get darker, retreat to the safety of your house. Now is the time to do some cocooning. If you feel hopeless from the spate of bad luck, sit out the month!

Education - *Work with others*
Not thrilling as your personal luck is at a low ebb. But although luck is poor, you can piggyback on the good luck of others, so jump on their bandwagon! Don't try to study alone if making no progress. Your pals are more than willing to help, and you will have every chance to repay the favour later.

12th Month
Jan 6th - Feb 3rd 2022

RELATIONSHIPS PLAY A BIGGER ROLE. ROMANCE BLOSSOMS.

Good fortune luck returns as you enter the new year, bringing happiness especially with relationships and affairs of the heart. A most romantic month! Whether you are yet to meet the love of your life, already have, or are happily married, there are countless special moments to savour and enjoy! An auspicious time to tie the knot and to take a relationship to the next level. Friendships get strengthened and whether focusing on your work, social life or love life, the people who make up your world matter more now than ever. Connections play a bigger part in your everyday life, so don't be a hermit. Mix, mingle, call on friends, socialize. There's a lot of joy, but also terrific new opportunities that come unexpectedly in the course of your socializing.

Work & Career - *Teamwork*

You regain career direction and see clearly how your future is shaping up even if earlier you may have been in a foggy situation. Not only are you able to make big decisions, you are armed with the knowledge you need to make the right choices. The loners among you who normally prefer working alone should try working with partners, as teamwork seems to augur more success and quicker rewards this month. Since love luck is on the ascent, be careful of office romances and careless liaisons, which may otherwise jeopardize a brilliant month!

Business - *Networking*

All goes well and all you need to do is just go a step further and work on business contacts, as relationships play a big role. If submitting a tender or contract, do it yourself as the opposite party is very receptive to dealing directly with you rather than with your subordinates. Work on broadening your network and prepare for someone from the past to contact you bringing business opportunities. Listen to all ideas and do not dismiss any that sound offbeat, as it could lead to big profits. Increase your networking efforts. Call up those you have not seen in a long time, be extra friendly, put in a personal touch in your dealings. All these little gestures do not cost much and take up relatively little time but will go a long way, so will be well worth the effort.

A good time to develop friendships as you find yourself having great affinity with just about everyone.

Love & Relationships - *Attuned to love*

A great month for love! Your mind is attuned to polishing up relationships. This month awakens the fantasist in you where you believe there's more to life than earning money. There's nothing better than having someone to share your newly realized revelations with. An especially good time for marriage proposals. Looking towards the future when your personal chi is so good bodes well for the longevity of the union. Singles meanwhile are particularly susceptible to romance and hot dates. If looking, you will meet many who attract and are attracted by you!

Home & Family - *Time for bonding*

You are happier than you've been in some time, so now is the best time to spread joy around. Make time to bond with the family, extended family included. Some pleasant surprises in store!

Education - *Exam luck*

You are able to concentrate and studying comes easier than usual. A little effort goes a long way! Projects and assignments get finished on time leaving you more time for your other interests. You can see the big picture easily and not get side-tracked by distractions. Those taking exams can look forward to excellent results.